Membership
Operations

CORE COMPETENCIES IN MEMBERSHIP MANAGEMENT

Membership Operations

EDITED BY

Diane C. Feirman, CAE

ASAE Membership Section

american society of
association executives

WASHINGTON, D.C.

Information in this book is accurate as of the time of publication and consistent with standards of good practice in the general management community. As research and practice advance, however, standards may change. For this reason, it is recommended that readers evaluate the applicability of any recommendation in light of particular situations and changing standards.

American Society of Association Executives
1575 I Street, NW
Washington, DC 20005-1103
Phone: (202) 626-2723
Fax: (202) 408-9634
E-mail: books@asaenet.org

George E. Moffat, Vice President, Marketing and Communications
Anna Nunan, Director of Book Publishing
Anthony Conley, Operations Coordinator
Jennifer Moon, Production Manager
Cover and interior design by Troy Scott Parker, Cimarron Design

This book is available at a special discount when ordered in bulk quantities. For information, contact the ASAE Member Service Center at (202) 371-0940.

A complete catalog of titles is available on the ASAE Web site at **www.asaenet.org/bookstore**

Library of Congress Cataloging-in-Publication Data

Membership operations / edited by Diane C. Feirman.
     p. cm. — (Core competencies in membership management)
    ISBN 0-88034-176-9
       1. Trade associations—Membership—Management. 2. Professional associations—Membership—Management. 3. Associations, institutions, etc.—Membership—Management. 4. Association marketing. I. Feirman, Diane C. II. American Society of Association Executives. III. Series.

  HD2421 .M46 2001
  060'.68'8—dc21

                            00-053109

Printed in the United States of America.
10 9 8 7 6 5 4 3 2 1

Contents

Preface

I**T IS OFTEN SAID**, and rightly so, that membership is the most important aspect of an association. Members are the reason the association exists and all of the association's activities are geared (or should be geared) toward addressing the needs of current and prospective members.

The importance of membership to associations makes it essential that staff responsible for membership issues are well educated and knowledgeable in the area of association management. Often, the focus is on recruiting and retaining members (selling the membership and the multiple aspects associated with the sell) and delivering membership benefits. These areas are important; however, one fundamental issue is frequently overlooked—the management responsibilities of the individual who directs the membership function for an association.

The membership manager or vice president or director (the title list is far-reaching) is a manager and a leader who is responsible for a number of key association management tasks, including pulling together and leading a staff, budgeting, managing the database, managing dues and benefit structures, managing volunteers, and keeping on top of legal issues. Although not strictly "membership" issues, these areas are an integral part of a successful association membership department (be it a department of one or twenty or more), and they should be addressed from a membership point of view. Indeed, frequently asked questions on the American Society of Association Executives (ASAE) Membership Section listserver center on these management areas and, more often than not, the answers can be hard to obtain.

It is for this reason that the ASAE Membership Section has included these management areas in its body of knowledge for the membership professional. In *Core Competencies in Membership Management: Membership Operations,* the second in a series of three books on the membership body of knowledge produced by the Membership Section Council, the focus is on providing an in-depth look at these management functions. Our goal is to fill in the knowledge gaps and provide the information on these areas that membership professionals need to know so they can manage these tasks in an exemplary manner and ensure success for their association's membership programs.

We hope this book serves to meet this goal and helps readers continue on their path to being successful association membership management professionals.

– Diane Feirman, CAE

CHAPTER ONE

Membership Director's Role and Responsibility

Kevin P. Corcoran

*"Membership is the lifeblood of **every** association."*

IF YOU HEAR THIS PHRASE ONCE, you will hear it a thousand times—because it is true. An association is no more than a collection of people or companies with similar interests. Without these people, there is no association. Although these individuals and organizations may benefit from the products and services your association offers, they may not know that they need them, recognize that you offer them, or be willing to make the investment in them without a persuasive argument. To keep your association's mission alive, you need to recruit these potential members and take active steps to retain the members you already have. For this reason, you, the membership director, could be considered the association's most important staff person.

The membership department is typically charged with recruiting, retaining, and satisfying members' needs. Although the size and scope of each individual association dictates which functions and responsibilities fall under the membership department, these duties are likely to include finding new members and holding on to current ones.

To successfully recruit and retain members, you must thoroughly understand the needs and interests of current and prospective members, conditions and trends within the industry or profession, and the association's products and services that address those needs and trends. Current or prospective members may ask for specific information about any number of association services. Although you are not expected to understand the intricacies of a complex conference or legislative position, you must be able to provide at least a preliminary answer. (You wouldn't expect a car salesperson to be able to explain exactly how anti-lock brakes work, but you would expect him or her to know if the car he sells has an anti-lock brake system.)

To gain this level of knowledge, you should develop strong working relationships with the other department directors. Membership is affected by every other department in the association, because each department creates and delivers the products that you sell to members and prospects. Similarly, the interactions that other association staff have with members can help inform you about the products and services that are most highly valued by members, helping you better focus your marketing and promotional efforts.

Staff interaction with members is a form of market research. The association's members are the best source for information concerning the services they value. Because members frequently do not know which staff person they should contact about a specific program, they may share valuable information about an existing or potential program with a staff person from an unrelated department. The challenge is to draw that information out of the member and get it to the staff person who can best use this knowledge. Information you need to help attract new members is often known by other staff members, but not communicated back to the membership department. Because this level of communication may be perceived by other staff as additional work, rather than an essential part of their job, the association chief executive officer (CEO) can be an invaluable resource for establishing and encouraging interdepartmental cooperation.

The CEO also can be your liaison to the association's board of directors. As elected leaders, board members are charged with shaping and determining the organization's long-term mission and direction. Understanding these big-picture issues is essential to successfully presenting it to prospective members. The nature of board–staff interaction varies significantly from one association to another, so be sure to follow appropriate protocol when communicating with or to board members.

By the same token, the membership department influences every other function within the organization. This department is often most closely attuned to the broad needs and interests of the association's members. Therefore, any significant additions, subtractions, or revisions to the association's line of products and services should be considered within the context of membership, and with the active participation of the membership director. You may be able to provide an understanding of the features and benefits of membership that are most highly prized by members. Frequently, the membership director is the first staff person to learn of an opportunity to create new offerings or to refine current ones to better suit members' needs. By acting as an information source to your fellow directors, you can foster interaction and cooperation. Without cooperation among departments, the quality and effectiveness of both the association's products and the promotional materials used to present them to the membership will suffer.

Your positive relationship with fellow staff is most important when you suggest to other directors new products or services that the association might develop. If you have a strained relationship with the other directors, they may be resistant to accepting suggestions from you. Opposition from other department directors can hamper the adoption of ideas, making their implementation less effective, and the association less responsive to members' needs.

Strong, cooperative relationships, on the other hand, will allow you to suggest ideas to other staff and encourage the exploration of these proposals. In this way, the initial suggestion can be further refined and either integrated into existing association programs or used to serve as the genesis of entirely new operational opportunities. Similarly, other staff may suggest more effective ways to present existing programs to members and prospects, encouraging new members to join and existing members to continue to support the association.

Because the membership department is at the center of the association's operations, the position of membership director is ideal for an individual seeking to best understand the overall operations of a nonprofit association. No other department has such a wide range of duties and responsibilities, or has as great an opportunity to affect the association's future. The membership director position also fosters the development and use of a wide range of skills. A single day might require you to use such diverse skills as market research, advertising development, customer service, database management, financial planning, communications, and team building with fellow staff members. This range of duties and responsibilities ensures that every day brings new challenges and opportunities to learn and excel.

Every association is structured according to its unique needs and capabilities. However, given the significant impact membership has on an association's operations, the membership director job is a position that is rightly placed on par with other department heads. Including the head of the membership department among other director-level staff encourages information exchange.

Although many associations are structured this way, some place the head of the membership department on a lower level, reporting to an executive-level staff member—the vice president of finance, marketing, or administration, for example. This approach creates a distance between membership and the association's other operational areas and forms barriers to the open discussion and cooperative efforts that foster creative ideas and solutions.

Strategic Planning

Although you must respond to the needs and interests of your association's members, your job should be more proactive than reactive. Membership recruitment and retention efforts should be based on a solid understanding of current and potential members' interests and activities and on the direction of the industry the association serves. In baseball, center fielders don't wait for the ball to land to pick it up. Rather, from the moment the ball is hit, they determine where the ball will go and run to that spot, so when the ball gets there, they are in position to catch it. Similarly, by undertaking market research, which can be as extensive as environmental scans, focus groups, and surveys or as simple as asking members what they want and need, you can position yourself to benefit from these developments—with recruitment programs in place—when the potential members arrive.

If a plan isn't already in place, the best source of knowledge to draw from when developing strategic plans is your current membership. Assemble a group of your current members with whom you can share ideas and gather insights. Whether these members are a formal membership committee or an informal group of advisers is largely up to you. Even if your board has appointed a membership committee, you may want to approach these or other members individually to seek their advice and guidance. Most members are honored to share their knowledge with you.

There are many ways to use an advisory council to refine your strategic planning and implementation. These include:

- *New sources of members*—Which niches of potential members are not currently being served? How do their needs or interests differ from those of your core members?

- *Repositioning current programs*—How can the association's existing products and services be repositioned to make them more attractive to current and potential members?

- *Marketing effectiveness*—What media and messages are most effective to capture potential members' attention? How can the association's marketing materials be refined to be more effective?

- *Industry trends*—What are the broad-based influences on the industry or profession your association serves? How are they changing the way your members live or work? What factors are affecting specific niches (geographic, demographic, and so forth) of the field, creating potential opportunities or threats?

- *Association strengths and weaknesses*—What does your organization do well? How could you better serve your industry? The staff and board may be too invested in current procedures and programs to fully understand these issues; members, with a more dispassionate view of the organization's operations, can provide a different perspective.

Your advisory committee also can help you manage internal issues, such as how to work with a difficult board member or association volunteer, or how to navigate the sometimes tricky political landscape within a nonprofit association. However, before you bring potentially touchy issues such as these to an adviser, be sure you're comfortable that he or she will respect and protect your confidence. There's no faster way to lose the confidence of your CEO and board than to be perceived as undermining their authority or being manipulative.

When, Why, and How to Outsource

Because your responsibilities are wide-ranging, sometimes the best way to get things done is to hire someone else to do it. Just as the association as a whole may transfer some tasks to outside vendors (for example, payroll processing, employee benefit management, Web site hosting and maintenance among others), you may be best served by hiring external companies or individuals to perform specific tasks or functions.

Outsourcing is often a way for associations to secure unique skills and resources without bringing a full-time person onto staff. It also can be a way to increase operational efficiency, particularly if the tasks to be outsourced are time consuming or do not contribute to the association's primary mission.

Far from being an admission of failure or inadequacy, outsourcing is often the most effective way to serve members. Tasks that may be candidates for outsourcing typically have one or more of the following characteristics:

- time consuming
- repetitive
- nonrevenue generating
- require specialized skills or equipment
- tangential relationship to the association's core purpose

This last item is particularly important. An association should not outsource a task that is essential to its mission. Outsourcing entails the loss of some level of control and is not appropriate for essential functions—areas where mistakes or failures can significantly harm the association's effectiveness, prestige, or financial health. For example, although the membership database is an essential asset for the organization because it contains all contact information about the association's members and customers, manually typing names and address information is not a core function. Similarly, creating printed material may be a mission-critical activity, but mailing these publications when they are ordered is not.

Once you've decided you want to outsource a task, you need to select your business partner. This individual or firm will act like an employee of the association and must be selected with the same level of care used to seek and hire a staff person. Keep in mind that the vendor will be working remotely, with limited oversight and with its other clients also laying claim to its time and attention.

You should interview a potential outsourcing partner just as you would a potential employee, asking many of the same questions, such as:

- How long have you been an outsourcing vendor?
- What is your level of experience performing the specific tasks that are being contracted for (particularly with associations)?
- Will adding us as a client adversely stretch your existing staff and/or equipment resources?
- How will the tasks be performed?
- What is your response time for standard and rush requests?
- What are your minimum standards for quality and accuracy?
- What is your method and frequency of communication?
- How many individuals within the firm will work on this account?
- What are the other resources available to the association, should the contact(s) be sick, take vacation, or leave the company?
- What will be the association's recourse should you fail to meet standards?

In general, your partner should have one or more staff who serve as the primary contact, dedicated (if the workflow allows) to the account, with additional staff cross-trained to assist in times of heavy workflow or the primary contact's absence.

Once you have interviewed a few companies and have found at least one with which you are comfortable, ask for a list of references. Contact the references and ask them how the vendor performs in reference to the questions listed above. The vendor's performance for its current clients is usually indicative of how it will work for your organization.

Ask the references probing questions, and listen to the message between the lines—a client may not want to report the negatives in its relationship, for fear that it will get back to the vendor and damage their relationship. To address this issue, ask potential vendors for names of former clients and the reasons why they no longer work with them—former clients are more likely to share negative information.

Finally, when all the references have been checked, listen to your "gut feeling." If something doesn't feel right, or there are still some unanswered questions, follow up by requesting more information or exclude that vendor from consideration. When hiring an individual, he or she can, to some extent, be molded to conform to the association's needs. An outsourcing partner is an independent company and is much harder to change to suit your needs.

Remember that your association is turning over a portion of its operations to an external company that may have many clients. Although the vendor will try to reflect your association's culture as much as possible, the nature of its "outsider" status makes a perfect match virtually impossible. Furthermore, as just one of a number of clients, your association will not receive the undivided attention of your vendor partner. On the other hand, when expectations and contract terms are explicitly stated, a relationship with an outsourcing partner is much easier to terminate than one with an employee.

Conclusion

Membership directors play a critical role in the success of their associations, not only through their ability to recruit and retain paying members, but also by sharing with other staff their insights and knowledge of members' needs and interests, thus helping to refine the association's offerings in all operational areas. The chapters that follow explore in more detail some of the operational aspects of the membership function and some specific skills that help membership directors perform at their best.

Kevin P. Corcoran is the executive vice president of the National Association of Health Underwriters (NAHU). He oversees all day-to-day functions of NAHU, which operates with 20 full-time staff personnel and a $3.5 million-dollar budget.

Prior to joining NAHU, he was the director of marketing for Georgetown University's Auxiliary Services Department, where he coordinated the marketing for on-campus business operations, which generated annual revenues of over $26 million.

CHAPTER TWO

Staffing the Membership Department

Tangie Newborn; Susan Nicolais, CAE; and Wes Trochlil

WHERE DO MEMBERS AND NONMEMBERS go when they have questions about their association? Who is the first person they talk to? The first contact many members and prospective members have is with someone in the membership department. This is where members form their first, and often long-lasting, impression of the association.

Essential Staff of the Association

Because associations are member-based organizations, staff that work most intimately with members need to be highly competent and responsive. Not only do these individuals represent the association to members but they also form the foundation for the entire association staff. Members often don't know whom to contact about specific issues, so the request goes to the membership department. By providing membership staff with information on all of the activities in the association, the association provides its members instantaneous service and keeps them coming back for more. Recruiting and developing competent membership staff is vital to the growth of membership and thus the success of the association.

The relationship of the membership director to the executive office reflects the importance placed on the membership function within the association. (See Sample Organizational Chart, page 13.) This recognition emphasizes to other staff the importance of the membership function within the association. It also lays the foundation for other staff to build on when dealing with members and prospective members who may have contacted them about a specific issue but have other questions. By emulating the membership staff, other staff can provide feedback members require without pushing them off to someone else. The "that's not my job, let me transfer you to someone else" mentality can be a quick way to alienate members and create barriers to open communication among the staff. Every staff person is a representative of the association and should respond in a timely fashion to members, even if it's to tell them they don't have the answer right now but they will get it for them.

Membership Staff

Some associations have multiple staff to perform the various functions of membership, while others may have one or two staff people to do everything. The size of the membership staff depends on the emphasis and resources of the association. In some associations, the emphasis will be on education; others may emphasize government relations or membership.

There are numerous positions that fall under the membership umbrella; these positions vary widely from association to association. No matter how large or small the membership staff, most associations will have at least two key positions—membership manager or director and data entry staff. In small associations, the data entry staff may perform additional duties, with the upkeep of member records the primary duty. The membership manager or director then does all the other work, including providing the leadership and vision for the department.

Regardless of the size, scope, or emphasis of the association, the core functions performed by the membership department remain the same: recruitment, retention, customer service, database maintenance, and marketing.

Sample Organizational Chart—
NNA Staff Organization (as of February 1, 2000)

EVP & CEO

Mgr. Board & Field Support

Recept./Mail Supervisor

VP, Govt. Relations & GC

Asst. Mgr., GR

VP, Mbrship & Meetings

Asst. Dir. Special Proj.

Asst. Dir. Meetings

Mbr. Service Spec.

Mgr. Database/System

Membership Rep.

Mg. Ed., Pub Aux.

Dir. Sales & Adv.

Assoc. Editor

Acct. Exec.

Dir. of Acct. & Fin.

Acct. Assistant

- *Recruitment*—develop recruitment plans, identify target markets, design recruitment campaigns, track results, evaluate effectiveness of campaigns

- *Retention*—develop retention plans, use volunteers, track retention numbers

- *Customer service*—focus on how well the needs of the members are served and be prepared to answer questions on all facets of the association's activities

- *Database maintenance*—maintain member records and prospect records, use data entry guidelines

- *Marketing*—determine how best to get the association's products and services out to the target markets in addition to selling membership

When recruiting membership staff, determine the core competencies required for the association to get the job done, and recruit to fill those competencies.

Titles for specific positions in membership are as varied as associations. They range from assistant, coordinator, and specialist to manager, director, and vice president. Using position descriptions that clearly define the responsibilities of each position is critical to ensuring the success of the individuals recruited to fill the positions. The position descriptions shown on pages 21–29 are just a sample of the various titles and responsibilities that fall under the purview of the membership department.

Outsourcing—An Extension of Staff

What do you do when the resources just aren't there to have the number of staff needed to get the job done? How about outsourcing? Many associations outsource noncore functions of the membership department to help an overworked staff. Outsourcing allows an association to use consultants and vendors to supplement its staff when adding additional staff members is not an option. If the association has limited resources, outsourcing allows associations to do more with less.

Areas that are good prospects for outsourcing range from designing brochures to telemarketing to fulfilling orders. Whenever an activity is outsourced, the association professional should maintain control throughout the project. Outsourcing doesn't relieve association professionals of responsibility for the project; they still have to work closely with the outside consultants to maintain quality control and get the job done.

Professional Development and Training

Membership professionals must work at continually improving their body of knowledge and understanding about membership development and association management. Depending on the level of experience, there is a broad array of professional development opportunities available to membership professionals. These opportunities are not limited to the traditional, full-day sessions with speakers. Professionals searching for continuing education and professional development have the option of taking courses via the Internet, CD, videotape, audiocassette, or audio conference.

Entry Level

Because the skill sets needed for an entry-level membership position are so broad, the offerings of continuing education and training for this area are equally broad. Entry-level membership professionals should develop skills in areas such as:

- the function of associations
- the use of standard software packages
- customer service and phone etiquette
- how to manage multiple tasks and deadlines
- data processing
- business writing
- basic marketing

Because these skills apply to professions beyond association membership positions, there are a multitude of sources from which membership professionals can choose to get this training. Groups like CareerTrack, the American Management Association, and others offer a wide variety of basic and advanced training courses.

In addition to these broad management courses, educational tracks focusing on association-specific issues are also available. Groups like the American Society of Association Executives (ASAE), the Greater Washington Society of Association Executives (GWSAE), and other ASAE-allied societies sponsor programs throughout the year for beginners through seasoned professionals.

Middle Management

As the membership professional's career progresses, he or she will find that a membership manager needs specific skills to continue to do the job effectively. Beyond the basic skills outlined above, membership managers should add the following skill sets to their repertoire:

- managing staff
- preparing and managing a budget
- developing and executing a membership acquisition and retention plan

With this more specialized skill set, membership professionals will find that the general business training mentioned above would suffice, as long as the focus is on how they will apply what they learn to their particular association experience. If their training and education are focused on the for-profit world, association professionals will have to "translate" what is being taught to their nonprofit reality.

Director

In addition to skill sets described above, the membership director will also need to develop skills in:

- understanding the industry the association serves
- understanding and identifying strategic issues for the membership and the association
- managing the board and volunteer committees

At this point, membership professionals rely more on ASAE and its allied societies for continuing education and professional development. Because these skill sets are so specific to associations, membership professionals will find that these skills can be learned only from experience, and programs addressing these skills are covered by a limited number of providers such as ASAE and its allied societies.

For example, ASAE offers a variety of specialized training sessions for experienced membership professionals. Among these are the Strategic Leadership Forum, ASAE's Annual Meeting and Exposition, the M&T (management and technology) conference, the School of Association Management, and the Future Leaders conference. In addition, the Greater Washington Society of Association Executives offers higher-level programs, such as its Navigator and Technology Solution Series.

Coaching for Quality Staff

In addition to keeping the members, volunteers, and senior management satisfied, membership directors also are responsible for ensuring that membership staff is the best it can be. Often, a candidate with all of the qualifications required for a position is difficult to find or a candidate is a great fit with the rest of the staff but may be lacking in some of the required skills. To help membership staff reach their full potential and thus have the department perform at optimum levels, the membership director is called on to be a coach and counselor.

Coaching helps staff focus on their knowledge and skills and how they can improve them. As a supervisor, the membership director works with employees through coaching to identify areas that need improvement, opportunities to get the needed training for improvement, and the results desired. When focusing on an employee's knowledge and skills through coaching is not enough, the membership director may need to become a counselor to help the employee look at behaviors and explore ways of altering the behaviors to ensure optimum performance.

Networking—Learning by Osmosis

Finally, all levels of membership professionals benefit by associating with their peers in the association community, as well as the members of their own association, through either formal or informal networking opportunities. Membership professionals should seek out other association professionals to learn from their experiences. Formal opportunities to network include the ASAE membership section listserver, ASAE and allied society events, and events sponsored by the membership professional's own association. The best informal opportunity is to simply pick up the phone or e-mail a colleague. Most association professionals understand the need to work with each other and to learn from each other, and all association professionals should take advantage of this opportunity.

Specializing in Membership

One might assume from the title that the membership specialist, be they coordinator, manager, or director, will focus exclusively on membership promotion and retention. For most membership professionals, however, this is far from accurate.

Because of the broad definition of "membership," the membership specialist may find that a multitude of other tasks fall into his or her domain. This may be especially true at associations with smaller staffs. Included among the areas likely to fall into the membership specialist's domain are:

- *Marketing*—This applies not only to marketing membership in the association, but also marketing the association's other products and services. This could range from promoting the association's books, audiotapes, and videotapes, to marketing seminars and continuing education programs.

- *Customer service*—If the association offers a wide variety of products and services, or for some other reason handles a large quantity of incoming calls, a customer service center may be appropriate. The customer service center frequently falls under the auspices of the membership department.

- *Meeting planning*—As the membership professional becomes more involved with board and volunteer management, the membership professional may need to plan and execute meetings.

- *Education*—Because membership professionals are in constant touch with their members, they may be called on to help develop educational programming offered by the association or in conjunction with other associations.

- *Communications*—With the variety of communication vehicles now coming from most associations (printed newsletters, e-mail newsletters, Web sites, and so forth), membership professionals are likely to be involved in some aspect of the association's communications, be it writing, editing, soliciting articles, or something else.

- *Public relations*—Talking with reporters or the general public may be required of the membership specialist, especially if the association represents a high-profile or controversial constituency.

- *Government relations*—If the association participates in lobbying activities or provides expert testimony in state or national legislatures, supporting these activities may fall to the membership specialist.

- *Chapters*—Frequently, associations will have chapters, and these chapters may be volunteer-led. Because the members of the chapters are (typically, though not always) members of the larger association, the duties of chapter management often fall to the membership department.

Summary

The duties of the association membership professional extend far beyond simply acquiring and retaining members. The membership staff represents the association to members and thus is tantamount in forming members' perceptions of the association. The skill set required to handle the myriad responsibilities in today's membership position is broad and deep. Staffing for the ideal membership department in today's labor market is a challenge complicated by the fact that the specialist in membership needs a broad range of skills.

RESOURCES

Books

Ferrett, Sharon K. *Positive Attitudes at Work*. Burr Ridge, Ill.: Irwin Professional Publishing, Mirror Press, 1994.

Jones, Bob. *How to Keep and Motivate Staff Specialists*. Washington, D.C.: ASAE Foundation, 1993.

Lucas, Robert W. *Coaching Skills: A Guide for Supervisors*. Burr Ridge, Ill.: Irwin Professional Publishing, Mirror Press, 1994.

Roderer, Phyllis, and Sandra Sabo, ed. *Human Resource Management in Associations*. Washington, D.C.: American Society of Association Executives, 1994.

Training courses

CareerTrack
www.careertrack.com, 1-800-488-0928.

American Management Association
www.ptseminars.com, 1-800-255-4141.

Database/System Manager—
Sample Position Description

**NNA
POSITION DESCRIPTION**

POSITION IDENTIFICATION:

Position Title: Database/System Manager

Department: Membership   **FLSA:** Exempt   **Date:** 4/19/98

SUPERVISORY RELATIONSHIPS:

Reports To: Vice President of Membership

Supervises: N/A

GENERAL DESCRIPTION: Maintain the NNA computer system. Trouble-shoot system problems and devise solutions. Maintain the integrity of the membership database. Serve as liaison with hardware and software consultants. Update member and prospective member information. Prepare and mail membership renewal notices. Work closely with the member services specialist to ensure proper credit is given for dues payment. Respond to requests for changes in circulation and dues. Produce mail merge letters, statistical reports, and financial reports for membership department and other departments as requested. Respond to member requests in a timely manner.

MAJOR DUTIES:

Maintain the NNA computer system. Trouble-shoot system problems and work with outside vendors to develop solutions as needed. Anticipate future needs of NNA in the computer system. Perform routine maintenance procedures such as backup and schedule regular maintenance on the system. Maintain the necessary inventory supplies, such as toner cartridges and paper for the computer system. Work with the staff to ensure that adequate training on computer programs is available.

Maintain the accuracy of the membership database. Utilize various sources of information, including directories of newspapers, to validate the accuracy of the database. Input changes to member records. Ensure that no duplicate memberships exist. Prepare membership and subscription renewal notices and the corresponding letter. Work with staff and temporary help to ensure notices are sent on schedule. Perform database maintenance. Work closely with software consultant to ensure the database is working at optimum level.

Produce membership reports to analyze the cash flow and retention rate for membership income. Design new reports to meet the needs of the organization.

Continues on next page

Continued from previous page

Prepare mailing labels, reports and mail merge documents for all departments as requested. Produce the mailing list for *Publishers' Auxiliary*. Write the reports and prepare the files for production of the membership directory.

Manage the broadcast fax program. Produce lists for sending faxes. Send materials to the vendor for faxing. Notify requestor when materials have been sent. Maintain the broadcast fax log and keep it available for accounting to verify charges. Serve as staff liaison with the broadcast fax vendor.

Serve as a contact for information on NNA membership. Respond to requests for information and changes in a timely manner. Assist the Executive Vice President and Director of Membership as needed. Participate in cross-functional teams to ensure the success of NNA projects.

REQUIRED KNOWLEDGE, SKILLS, AND ABILITIES:

The position requires:
- ➢ Knowledge of LAN networks and network administration.
- ➢ Knowledge of membership databases, preferably TASS and their maintenance.
- ➢ Knowledge of Microsoft Word, Excel, and PowerPoint, Internet, and email.
- ➢ Strong organizational skills and the ability to handle multiple projects.
- ➢ Excellent analytical skills, written and oral communication skills, and customer service skills.
- ➢ Ability to work with minimal supervision.
- ➢ Ability to maintain good interpersonal relationships.
- ➢ Ability to work with volunteer leaders.
- ➢ Ability to work with outside contractors.

EMPLOYMENT STANDARDS:

The position requires any combination of education, experience, and training equivalent to:
- ➢ Bachelor's degree.
- ➢ 3 years of experience with at least 2 years in association database and network administration.

Member Service Representative—
Sample Position Description

NNA
POSITION DESCRIPTION

POSITION IDENTIFICATION:

Position Title: Member Service Representative

Department: Membership **FLSA:** Non-Exempt **Date:** 10/06/99

SUPERVISORY RELATIONSHIPS:

Reports To: Vice President of Membership

Supervises: N/A

GENERAL DESCRIPTION: Serve as the primary contact for member queries. Make telephone contact with members prior to mailing of member profile sheet and prior to expiration of membership. Respond to member calls and provide information to members immediately or within 24 hours of requests. If unable to handle the call, route to appropriate staff using a call routing form. Follow-up on calls routed to other staff within 24 hours. Keep call log of calls received in the voice mail system. Serve as the assistant to the Executive Director of the National Newspaper Association Foundation for 10 hours per week.

MAJOR DUTIES:

Serve as the primary telephone contact for member calls. Provide members with the information requested. Maintain files on all association activities to enable you to respond to member calls. If unable to provide a response, route the call to the appropriate staff person using the call routing form. Maintain responsibility for the resolution of all routed calls. Follow up with the appropriate staff person to ensure they have responded to the member.

Make initial telephone contact with members prior to the mailing of the member profile. Verify the information contained in the profile. Solicit input from members on the performance of NNA. Provide immediate follow-up to any problems or complaints. Make telephone contact with members whose membership has expired. Solicit input from members on the reasons for non-renewal of membership. Keep log of reasons why membership was not renewed.

Continues on next page

Continued from previous page

Enter basic changes into member records as time allows while member is on the phone. When complex changes are required, enter changes on the record change request form and submit to data entry.

Use the telephone contact with members to gather data that will assist NNA in meeting the needs of members. Maintain a call log of all calls received in voice mail. Provide weekly reports to immediate supervisor.

Assist the Executive Vice President of the National Newspaper Association Foundation with general clerical and correspondence for 10 hours per week.

Assist the Director of Membership and the membership department as needed. Participate in cross-functional teams to ensure the success of NNA projects.

REQUIRED KNOWLEDGE, SKILLS, AND ABILITIES:

The position requires:
➢ Excellent written and oral communication skills, and customer service skills.
➢ Knowledge of membership databases.
➢ Knowledge of Microsoft Word, Excel, Internet, and email.
➢ Strong organizational skills and the ability to handle multiple projects.
➢ Ability to work with minimal supervision.
➢ Ability to maintain good interpersonal relationships.
➢ Ability to work with volunteers.

EMPLOYMENT STANDARDS:

The position requires any combination of education, experience, and training equivalent to:
➢ Bachelor's degree.
➢ 3 years of experience with at least 1 year in the association environment.

Member Services Specialist—
Sample Position Description

**NNA
POSITION DESCRIPTION**

POSITION IDENTIFICATION:

Position Title: Member Services Specialist

Department: Membership   **FLSA:** Non-Exempt   **Date:** 6/22/99

SUPERVISORY RELATIONSHIPS:

Reports To: Vice President of Membership

Supervises: N/A

GENERAL DESCRIPTION: Update member and prospective member information. Process dues payments. Produce and mail membership renewal notices and membership press cards. Pay membership dues and event registrations in membership database. Respond to requests for changes in circulation and dues. Provide marketing and administrative support to the membership department. Enter meeting registration information into system. Administer the NNA product and publication sales program. Fulfill membership and meeting information requests. Assist the Assistant Director of Meetings with general correspondence. Respond to member requests in a timely manner.

MAJOR DUTIES:

Maintain the accuracy of the membership database. Enter new members into the database. Input changes to member and nonmember records. Process dues payments. Research payments, make corrections, and balance entries. Run cleanup reports and correct errors in data entry. Utilize various sources of information, including directories of newspapers, to validate the accuracy of the database.

Prepare membership and subscription renewal notices and the corresponding letter. Ensure notices are sent on schedule. Mail the membership press cards and press stickers. Fulfill requests for information on membership. Interact with members via phone, fax, email and correspondence as necessary.

Administer the NNA publication and product sales program. Maintain inventory and sales records. Fulfill order requests. Serve as point of resolution for member problems with products and publications. Provide supervisor with monthly reports.

Continues on next page

Continued from previous page

Enter meeting registrations into the database. Fulfill requests for information on meetings. Stuff meeting registration packets. Provide support for general correspondence in the meetings department.

Assist the Director of Membership and the membership department as needed. Participate in cross-functional teams to ensure the success of NNA projects.

REQUIRED KNOWLEDGE, SKILLS, AND ABILITIES:

The position requires:
➢ Knowledge of relational membership data bases, preferably TASS.
➢ Knowledge of Microsoft Word, Excel, and PowerPoint, Internet, and email.
➢ Strong organizational skills and the ability to handle multiple projects.
➢ Excellent written and oral communication skills.
➢ Excellent customer service skills.
➢ Ability to work with minimal supervision.
➢ Ability to maintain good interpersonal relationships.

EMPLOYMENT STANDARDS:

The position requires any combination of education, experience, and training equivalent to:
➢ Associate's degree.
➢ 2 years of experience with at least 1 year working with association databases.

Vice President of Membership and Meetings— Sample Position Description

**NNA
POSITION DESCRIPTION**

POSITION IDENTIFICATION:

Position Title: Vice President of Membership & Meetings

Department: Membership   **FLSA:** Exempt   **Date:** 2/03/00

SUPERVISORY RELATIONSHIPS:

Reports to: Executive Vice President & CEO

Supervises: Assistant Director, Meetings
Assistant Director, Special Projects
Database/systems Manager
Customer Service Representative
Member Services Specialist

GENERAL DESCRIPTION: Manage the membership programs including production of the NNA Membership Directory, Annual Convention and Government Affairs Conference. Prepare and implement a membership development plan including recruitment and retention. Develop and implement methods of tracking membership statistics. Ensure the integrity of the membership database. Work to improve the relationship with affiliate and partner state associations. Develop and monitor departmental budgets. Manage the member affinity programs. Schedule special work activities for the department. Supervise membership department staff. Establish annual departmental goals and objectives. Serve as staff liaison for the Membership Committee and Member Services Committee. Support the GAC and Annual Convention Committee. Identify new non-dues revenue sources. Represent NNA at conferences and meetings. Assist the Executive Vice President as needed.

CRITICAL ELEMENTS:

Manage the functions of the membership department. Develop membership marketing programs. Determine target markets for promotional activities. Recruit new members. Maintain the integrity of the membership database. Track monthly membership statistics. Develop and implement retention plan. Serve as a direct point of contact for members. Respond to member requests in a timely fashion. Work closely with the Membership Committee. Make recommendations to the committee on needed changes

Continues on next page

Continued from previous page

to procedures. Prepare and distribute committee agendas and minutes. Participate in committee meetings. Coordinate the activities of the NNA State Chairmen. Develop member surveys. Serve as point of resolution for membership issues. Work with outside vendor to develop and produce the membership directory.

Manage the member affinity programs. Identify new products and services to offer to members. Negotiate contracts with potential affinity providers.

Work to enhance the relationship with the affiliate and partnership state press associations. Develop plan to move affiliate states to a partnership status. Serve as the primary point of contact for state press associations. Attend state press associations meetings to represent NNA. Provide NNA resource materials to state press associations for distribution at their meetings. Facilitate communication between NNA and the state press associations.

Evaluate and implement new member services. Work closely with the Member Services Committee. Make recommendations to the committee on needed changes to programs. Prepare and distribute committee agendas and minutes. Participate in committee meetings. Identify additional sources of non-dues revenue. Negotiate contracts for new affinity programs. Monitor the contracts of all affinity programs. Review contracts and programs on a periodic basis to determine the feasibility of continuing the program.

Oversee the planning of the Government Affairs Conference and the Annual Convention. Participate in contract negotiations and site visits. Assist as needed in preparation for these meetings. Participate in cross-divisional teams to ensure the success of the meetings. Attend Board of Directors meetings as directed. Prepare department report for presentation at the Board meetings.

Develop budgets for membership department including dues income, awards program, meetings and member services. Monitor the budget activity on a monthly basis. Review supporting detail for all department expenses.

Supervise the membership department staff. Set goals and objectives for the department and individual staff members. Conduct periodic staff reviews. Serve as a mentor for staff.

Participate in the Management Team. Attend team meetings. Participate in cross-divisional teams as needed. Assist the Executive Vice President as requested.

REQUIRED KNOWLEDGE, SKILLS, AND ABILITIES:

The position requires:
➢ Knowledge of membership databases, membership marketing, developing and managing member services, strategic planning, and budget process.

Continued from previous page

> - Excellent management skills, oral and written communication skills, and customer service skills.
> - Knowledge of Microsoft Word, Excel, and PowerPoint.
> - Ability to prioritize multiple projects, work in a fast paced environment, and meet deadlines and budget projections.
> - Ability to work with volunteer leaders and with committees.
> - Ability to maintain good interpersonal relationships.

EMPLOYMENT STANDARDS:

Any combination of education, experience, and training equivalent to:
> - Master's Degree.
> - 8 years of experience in association membership development with at least 3 years experience working with committees desired.

Tangie Newborn is interim executive director for the
National Association of Black Journalists (NABJ), a professional association located in Adelphi, Maryland. Before joining
NABJ, Newborn served as deputy executive director of the
American Medical Women's Association. She has 17 years of
association management experience with emphasis in membership marketing, program development, and fundraising.

Newborn has written many articles and developed training sessions on membership development and retention, time management, and team building. She presently
serves on the Membership Section Council of the American Society of Association
Executives (ASAE) and is the past president of the Perrywood Community
Association.

Susan Nicolais, CAE, has over 15 years' experience in associations and is currently
vice-president of Membership and Meetings for the National Newspaper Association.
Nicolais is active in the American Society of Association Executives (ASAE) and
the Greater Washington Society of Association Executives (GWSAE). She was
executive editor of the *Membership Marketing* handbook (ASAE 2000) and presently
serves on the ASAE Membership Section Council as chairman and on the GWSAE
Certified Association Executive Advisory Council. Nicolais received an MA in
Human Resource Development from Marymount University in Arlington, Va.

Wes Trochlil is president of Effective Database Management
(EDM) in Fairfax, Va. Trochlil is an independent consultant
providing associations with a variety of services for association
management systems, including selection, implementation,
project management, documentation, and training. Before
founding EDM, he was vice president of McKinley Marketing, Inc., a consulting firm that provides affinity marketing
programs to associations. Trochlil has nearly ten years of association management
experience and has served as director of membership, marketing, and customer
service for the National Association of College and University Business Officers,
the Food and Drug Law Institute, and the Food Processing Machinery & Supplies
Association. He is a frequent writer and speaker for the American Society of
Association Executives (ASAE), the Greater Washington Society of Association
Executives (GWSAE), and the Canadian Society of Association Executives (CSAE).

CHAPTER THREE

Dues and Benefits

Diana M. Ewert, MPA, CAE

ONE OF THE UNIQUE ASPECTS of our society is our willingness as individuals to rally around a common cause, goal, task, trade, or profession. There are as many organizations as there are causes, professions, hobbies, and interests. Each organization has its own way of classifying its members as well as reflecting its members' developmental stages.

The terms *classification* and *category* often are used interchangeably; however, in this chapter, the term *classification* is used in its broadest sense. Individual, corporate, associate, international, and virtual are member classifications. The term *category* is used to reflect a member's developmental stage within an organization. Thus, categories are used to further define the nature of the member relationship.

Classifications and categories are usually broadly defined in an organization's governing documents. Organization governing documents consist of the articles of incorporation and bylaws. Equally important are interpretations and definitions of the language used in operation manuals, board and association operating policies, and standard operating procedures. These documents outline the basic definitions of membership, define the parameters of membership (qualifications), and may explain member benefits. This chapter will discuss various member classifications and categories, define how they can be used, and allow for special considerations within each description.

Membership Classifications

Individual Membership Classifications

Individual membership is defined as a one-to-one relationship: one person, one membership. The nature and complexity of categories differ among organizations.

General members. General members are the primary stakeholders in an organization. In a trade organization, general members are most actively involved in the profession and usually pay a premium in membership dues. Within the general membership, there may be a further breakdown of membership types, such as regular membership or supplier or associate membership. Each membership type may have a different dues structure. Supplier or associate members may have voting privileges and rights, as do general members. In an educational organization, for example, general members are actively involved in the education of the profession that the organization represents. General members often serve as adjunct faculty and are used as educators in providing continuing education to the practicing community.

This personal monetary investment of dues paid to the organization follows their voluntary involvement in many areas of the association's management, such as governance, policy, advocacy, education, and research. General members are afforded all the rights and privileges as defined in the governing documents, including the right to vote and hold office. In a healthy association, general membership represents the largest member population. The general membership brings to an organization two vital and priceless resources: knowledge and time.

Student members. If general members are considered the mainstay of individual member organizations, then student members represent the greatest source of cultivation as members and as customers. Associations offer student members educational support and resources as well as career development and employment assistance.

Student membership is often subsidized by the organization. Student groups can be active in the organization, often serving as representatives on committees, boards, and task forces. Criteria for student membership vary greatly and depend on the profession. For example, a medical association may require that student members be enrolled in a medical degree program. The Golf Course Superintendents Association of America requires student members to be enrolled as full-time students (12 or more credit hours) in an approved turf-grass program. Student members represent the best opportunity for an association to cultivate a relationship that will continue beyond graduation.

Educator/faculty members. Educator and faculty membership also may be subsidized by the organization. Faculty who teach a curriculum in a specific industry or profession may be afforded a special dues rate. Criteria for a faculty membership may vary based on whether the educator is full-time faculty or an adjunct professor. The organization's governing documents should outline criteria for membership. One of the overlooked advantages to this membership category is the cultivation of a relationship with students. Educators and faculty members are familiar with the advantages of establishing a relationship with organizations for the purposes of furthering career objectives. This key membership class is integral to building a strong student member base, setting up a platform for cultivating long-term relationships with young, upcoming professionals.

International members. International membership is reserved for members who reside outside the country where the association is located. International members are actively involved in the profession, trade, or mission of the organization and qualify for general membership. Membership fees for international members depend on the benefits and services offered. Mailing fees for international members can be expensive. It is not unusual for organizations to offer international members reduced membership fees; however, trade publications are often not included as a member benefit. The cost of postage combined with the unreliable nature of postal delivery outside the United States makes electronic access not only more attractive, but more cost effective.

Associate members. The associate member classification is used for those interested in the organization—its profession, vision, and mission—whose business is unrelated to the organization, and who do not qualify for any other membership classification. Associate members are eligible for specified or limited benefits and, as a rule, are not eligible to vote. Because their involvement with the organization is peripheral, they are not considered stakeholders. Some examples of associate members could include a community library with an interest in architecture joining an architect society or a social service organization with an interest in psychiatry with membership in a mental health organization.

Organizational Member Classifications

Corporate members are most common in trade associations (organizations representing business or industry). Corporate members represent a business, partnership, or corporation actively engaged in the manufacture or supply of goods and services to a particular industry. The dues structure for corporate membership varies from organization to organization. It can be a lump-sum annual payment, with differing benefits depending on the level of membership selected. Corporate membership also can be calculated based on criteria such as annual sales, number of employees, or population served. Trade associations depend on corporate involvement to sustain individual membership programs, goods, and services.

Corporate member categories should be crafted so that corporate members can make a significant contribution to the association beyond promoting products and services. If corporate membership exists only to offer a means of promotion or sales, dues for this category may be considered taxable income by the Internal Revenue Service.

There is a distinct difference between associate and corporate membership. The business conducted by corporate members is directly related to the organization; however, the business conducted by associate members is unrelated.

Member Categories

Remember that a member class is a broad definition, whereas a member category is reflective of a developmental stage. An example of a membership class/category is a general/retired member. *General* indicates a general member (rather than an educator, supplier, or student), and *retired* indicates that the member is at the retirement stage of his or her career.

Special Members

Member categories can be used to meet specialized organizational needs, grant recognition, or edify the profession. Life, retired, inactive, honorary—each category reflects a special consideration accorded to each distinctive group.

Life Member

Life membership is usually conveyed to individuals who have spent a certain number of years as general or active members within the association. Some associations offer a lifetime membership for a lump sum payment. One of the benefits of this category is the elimination or reduction of dues. However, this can present a downside for the organization.

Associations are faced with an aging membership base. The financial impact of supporting a non- or reduced-fee membership category, such as life, can increase exponentially. This creates a dynamic whereby a weighted group can exert influence over association policy. For example, an organization with an aging membership base that no longer has a financial stake (nondues paying) in the organization may have limited voting privileges and electronic access to publications. It is important to review the criteria for life membership as well as the organization's demographic profile. Associations must be proactive and anticipate shifts in the membership base.

Some organizations also experience a stigma attached to life categories. Granting life membership based on years of involvement may be detrimental to those who consider themselves to be in the prime of their profession and feel they are still able to make valuable contributions.

Consider a member category that will allow these individuals to be valued for long-term membership and still view themselves as general members.

Retired Member

Retired membership recognizes those who have retired from the profession or industry, but who wish to remain active and continue to network with peers and colleagues. The benefits associated with this category reflect a reduction in fees and services. Criteria for this category may include a combination of age, income, and years of membership.

Inactive Member

There are times when maintaining membership in an association becomes difficult because of unemployment, illness, or other circumstance. These are the times when the services and benefits become even more important. An association may grant a member temporary inactive status and waive membership fees. Inactive membership is reviewed periodically, and the member is asked to requalify to maintain active status. This membership category may be administered by the membership committee or reviewed by the association board of directors. Other questions that should be answered dealing with benefits are: Is an inactive member eligible to vote? To receive publications? To participate in leadership roles? The answers will be found in the governing documents and policy manuals. If the organization is considering an inactive membership, defining the benefits of this class is critical.

Honorary Member

Honorary membership is a special category of membership used to recognize an individual who has been a supporter or advocate of the profession or has sustained a record of service. Associations traditionally use the honorary classification to edify the profession. Administration of this member category can be vested in an awards committee, a subcommittee of the board, or the membership committee. Honorary membership has no dues associated with the category. The true value to associations is the honor of a relationship with the individual named as a member.

Virtual or Electronic Member

Some associations provide Internet savvy members a means of becoming involved at their own time and pace. Using e-mail to push education and research materials, deliver publications, and provide a means of two-way communication with the organization, associations reduce the overhead costs associated with many traditional methods of service delivery. The concept of virtual membership is new to many organizations, but it is gaining in popularity, especially among early career and student members.

Member Benefits

What's in it for me? What is the value? What are the benefits? Associations are unique in that the value of membership must be communicated to recruit and retain members. Benefits are often structured according to the member classification and are further defined according to the member category. An individual member will have different benefits than will a corporate member, than will an associate member, than will an international member. (This assumes, of course, that the organization has multiple membership classifications. Some organizations offer only one class of membership.) Each group has specific needs and differing levels of involvement within the organization. Associations are tasked with developing a unique set of benefits for each classification that remains fluid and changes to meet the changing needs of the member class.

It would be impossible to provide a comprehensive listing of member benefits within the context of this chapter, especially given the broad array of affinity programs and nondues-related products and services. There is a wide range of tangible and intangible benefits. Tangible benefits are those the members can see and realize. Intangible benefits deal with the experience of being a member. Some examples of tangible benefits are:

- discounted fees for educational programs, publications, etc.
- access to members or a membership directory
- regular publications, such as a trade magazine

• discounts or group rates on programs, such as travel, insurance, legal advice, credit cards, long distance, Internet providers, etc.
• reciprocity (as negotiated) with other associations for member rates

Some examples of intangible benefits that are part of the membership experience include the opportunities to:

• vote, hold office, and serve on committees, councils, task forces
• present expert testimony to governing bodies
• participate in advocacy and legislative activities
• mentor a student or young career professional
• enhance the image of the organization and profession it represents
• educate the general public
• network with colleagues for career enhancement

General Members

General members are the mainstay of an association. Because they have the single largest investment in the organization in the form of the premium dues paid, general members qualify to vote, hold office, serve on committees, and receive discounted fees for educational programs, publications, etc.

The appointment of individuals to serve on the governance side of the organization may depend on the top elected official. However, it is not unusual for a combination of length of service, membership, and national and local activity to play a role in the selection process. In some organizations, general and corporate or supplier members may be equal in class and enjoy all the benefits of membership.

Membership advantages include discounted fees. Discounting for members is an accepted practice because membership dues and fees fund many of the association's programs and services. The American Psychiatric Association offers a member discount to its annual meeting that results in a savings of $400 over the nonmember rate. Additionally, publications offered through a subsidiary organization, American Psychiatric Press, Inc., also have member and nonmember rates.

Corporate/Supplier

These member benefits should be carefully structured. The benefits of membership must go beyond the opportunity to sell products and services. Corporate members are interested in furthering the industry or profession and can be offered unique opportunities to support the organization by sponsoring public relations and information outreach, research, and legislative or government relations activities. Other benefits of membership include discounted advertising rates; selection of exhibit space at trade shows; sponsorship of special events, including banquets and awards programs; and other activities that allow the association to allocate resources toward programs and services.

Associate

Because the associate member class is usually reserved for those with an interest in the association, the benefits of membership are limited. Access to information, publications, and some limited discounted fees are appropriate benefits. The associate member category is restricted when it comes to setting association policy. The right to vote and hold office is reserved for primary stakeholders—namely, general members.

International

Benefits of the international member category are also limited. International member fees are generally less than those of a general member. The opportunity to participate fully in the association is limited by geography, unless the association is affluent enough to support international travel or meetings. Providing publications to international members can be difficult. Mail delivery in countries outside the United States can be slow and expensive, is often misdirected, and can result in equally expensive returns. Address information can be difficult to verify. More associations are turning toward the Internet to meet the needs of international members. An international section of the organization's Web site, with access to online publications and journals, an opportunity to network with other members using chat rooms or bulletin boards, and online registration for annual meetings, is an effective and efficient way to deliver benefits to this member category.

To truly serve an international member population, an organization should translate some of its key materials, especially those that are not often revised (such as a membership application). Translation can be costly, however, and a market assessment or marketing plan should factor in the countries where the most return on investment can be realized. For example, if the organization has a market presence in Latin America and will be concentrating a recruitment effort because of the market potential, then translation of membership applications and educational program brochures may pay for itself. However, if the organization has a small presence in the Pacific Rim, the market is limited, and there is no concentrated recruitment effort in this region, it would be cost prohibitive to translate membership materials.

Virtual or Electronic Membership

The benefits of virtual membership are similar to those of international membership. The lower cost of a Web-based membership is justified because of cost savings in mailing, marketing, publications, and administration. There is, however, a caveat to Web-based membership. The start-up costs associated with an Internet enterprise can be expensive and depend on an organization's infrastructure. Outsourcing Web activities is becoming more common, but this also can be very expensive.

The New Membership Dynamic— Individualized Options

Associations are becoming more diverse. Member needs vary from age to culture to career plan to practice. Associations must heighten their awareness and review the benefits they offer against the benefits desired by their members. Members are becoming more astute and willing to trade off one benefit they may not use to gain another they would use consistently. Thus, an association may wish to consider offering a benefits cafeteria plan. Within the dues structure, members may select from programs or services that better meet their needs.

Let's say that General Member Bob, located in the Midwest, is heavily invested in his local organization. Bob values his association's trade journal, but has never attended an annual meeting and has no desire to participate in association governance. Bob regularly attends educational programs offered in his region and purchases quite a few texts from the association bookstore. The optimal membership benefit for Bob would be (1) the journal, (2) discounted regional education programs, and (3) certificates for textbooks.

General Member Joe, located in the Southeast, is heavily invested in the national organization, wouldn't miss an annual meeting, is computer savvy, and is considering running for a national office. Joe's optimal membership benefit is (1) online access to publications and (2) discounted annual meeting registration.

General Member Cheryl, on the West coast, has completed an advanced degree and is ready for a career move. Cheryl enjoys the journal and attends annual meeting and regional seminars for networking. She is not interested in serving the association as a volunteer, although she has been active within the special committee structure that deals with a specific issue. The membership benefits Cheryl prefers are (1) online access to publications, (2) discounts to educational programs and the annual meeting, (3) access to the association's job bank with career development assistance, and (4) the opportunity to remain active in her special interest area.

The cost of membership for each is the same. The difference is that membership fees are allocated according to each member's specific needs and special interests. The geographic boundaries that once defined each of these members are now obscured by technology—online offerings combined with face-to-face networking opportunities. This association is structuring member benefits to meet the needs of its members and is reallocating resources used to traditionally deliver information.

A cafeteria plan can be constructed using the member record as a base. The ideal situation would be to have members do so using Web-based technology. Not all organizations are this sophisticated, however. An organization can build the member information based on purchasing history, participation/registration at meetings, volunteer activity, etc., using database tables. The key is to use the member record as the platform for building the preferences.

Membership Renewal

Bill early, bill often. When it comes to renewing membership, this seems
to be the rule of thumb. Approximately six months before the member's
expiration date, database clean-up, record verification, and advance mail-
ings to qualify membership category all need to occur. Once the organization is reasonably confident in the integrity of its data, the renewal
process begins in earnest. All pertinent materials to be included with the
renewal are created parallel with data preparation. Information regarding
member benefits, an appeal to renew, and highlights of the association's
accomplishments during the previous year are appropriate.

The following steps are in general terms:

- Three months before expiration, the first notice is sent.
- The second notice is sent 30 days before expiration.
- Another notice is sent the month the membership actually expires.
- A past due notice is sent 30 days past expiration.
- Another past due notice is sent 60 days past expiration.
- A final or drop notice is sent at 90 days past expiration.

A nonrenewing member receives a total of six renewal notifications.
The first notice includes all the appeal information. The second usually
includes some targeted marketing information. The third may be just
a notice. The fourth notice includes another appeal and information
about the loss of benefits. The fifth will again hold an appeal letter as
well as highlight a specific program or benefit. The final or drop notice
should include an expression of what the loss in membership means to
the organization as well as an exit survey that will allow the organization
to assess the reason for nonrenewal. The notifications may be sent via
mail, e-mail, fax, or a personal telephone call.

Associations differ in renewing procedures and processing. Some
organizations bill according to the anniversary date or the date a
member record is created. Other organizations use an annual billing
date—the same date for everyone each year. In both scenarios, members
get accustomed to looking for the renewal form at a specific time of the
year. Each has advantages and disadvantages.

Annual versus Anniversary

Annual dues renewal allows an organization to know, before the start of the fiscal year, how much dues revenue can be allocated to programs and services. If an association's fiscal year runs from January 1 to December 31, the dues renewal process begins in early July and is completed in March. The association has a good idea of income by the end of December as well as a projection in savings in the potential drop population. One benefit of annual versus anniversary is projection and analysis. Another benefit is that the organization can plan for the additional staff required to process renewal returns. The annual renewal process is both efficient and effective.

A disadvantage to annual renewals is the complicated proration of dues for individuals who join the organization at times outside the renewal process. Members may become confused when they receive an odd dues notice.

Renewals based on anniversary date also have advantages. This type of renewal generates income for the association year round and relieves the burden of processing a flood of renewals over a compressed period. The renewal process becomes an ongoing effort.

There are several disadvantages to this. Marketing materials are ordered when needed throughout the year. Billings vary from month to month. Membership drops occur each month during the year and are reflected in fluid membership counts. Projections, although not impossible, are more difficult to obtain.

Several associations are beginning to explore and use multiple-year memberships, in which a member can pay one lump sum for the next several years of membership in advance (often at a discounted rate). This can have several benefits for individual members (including removing the responsibility of remembering to renew and the financial benefit) as well as the association (it can enhance renewal rates by ensuring renewals for several years and reduce billing costs). However, as with all billing methods and dues structures, its viability must account for the nature of the association and its members.

Selecting the proper method for renewal depends on many factors. Is the association's accounting structure based on cash or accrual? Does the organization depend on membership revenue to fund other programs that occur later in the fiscal year? Is membership revenue shared with component organizations, such as regions or chapters? Does the organization have a history of better collections and cash flow in May than in December?

When Dues Rise

The rising costs of printed materials and postal rates, an increase in member benefits, or a special program enacted by the organization's board can all result in a dues increase. Associations determine what will be more beneficial: the incremental increase; smaller amounts over time to offset increasing costs; or a one-time, large increase earmarked to fund specific benefits or programs.

Once an increase is approved, the organization must sell the increase to its membership, especially if the increase is large. A direct correlation between the cost and benefit of program can be effective. This is especially true if the benefit is one that members have been requesting. Dues increases that are less tangible to the membership are more difficult to sell. Perhaps the association has decided to implement a public relations campaign to enhance the image of the profession. Perhaps the organization is moving into a more active advocacy role. There are no immediate or demonstrable benefits to implementing these types of programs.

The organization should plan a campaign to introduce the increase and educate the membership as to the rationale behind the decision as well as an indication of exactly (if possible) how the funds will be allocated. Staff should be educated to answer questions from members.

Planning for the Future

The evolving nature of membership is changing. This is due in large part to technological advances that have increased the speed of response. Mail has given way to fax, which in turn has given way to e-mail. For most associations, the traditional membership base is aging, and it is imperative that thought be directed toward the dynamic of a younger, enthusiastic member who has no vested interest in any organization beyond the instant gratification that is obtained in cyberspace.

Many associations are behind the Internet learning curve and are trying hard to catch up. Reserves are being used as technology investment capital. The future of membership organizations as they exist today will be different tomorrow; the only constant in this paradigm is change itself. Associations need to be more in tune with the demands of the generation and must balance these needs against the traditional membership base, which has sustained the membership activities of the past.

Organizations can plan for the future by capitalizing on the talents of members themselves. Early career and student members have grown up with the Internet and can offer associations powerful insight into the implementation and use of this tool. Life members have a perspective that only maturity and longevity in the profession can bring. Associations must continue to appreciate the rich history and tradition reflected in the membership. General members have a unique opportunity to manage both groups for the good of the association in the here and now and into the future. Associations that keep checking the pulse of their membership will be able to celebrate the past and embrace the future.

Diana M. Ewert, MPA, CAE, started her association management career in 1992. She has worked with philanthropic, trade, social service, and education organizations. Ewert received a master's degree in public administration–nonprofit management from the Bloch School of Business, University of Missouri–Kansas City. In 1999, she received the Certified Association Executive designation. Ewert is the managing director for member and customer operations, (United States and Europe) for the Urban Land Institute in Washington, D.C. She is the chair of the ASAE Chapter Relations Section Council and has served as a member on the ASAE Ethics Committee.

CHAPTER FOUR

Records Management and Database Issues

Wes Trochlil, Michael Connor, and Loretta DeLuca

DATA MANAGEMENT SYSTEMS, otherwise known as association management systems (AMS), are a significant investment. This centralized system essentially manages the organization's day-to-day operations, including membership application and dues renewal, meeting logistics and registration, product sales, certification tracking, contact management and activity tracking, reporting, and more.

According to *Association Technology Trends* (American Society of Association Executives, 1997), more than 40 percent of 1,185 association survey respondents have a centralized database. An AMS is able to track and access real-time information across functional areas. It allows the association to develop an in-house "standard" of consolidated, thorough demographic- and activity-related data on all member and nonmember records, thereby improving its ability to market and deliver relevant services. A centralized, multifunctional system streamlines operations, reduces duplication of effort, consolidates isolated data, and ultimately enhances staff productivity. In addition, many market offerings have integrated Web modules that allow members to post updates, order products, register for meetings, and more, all with a direct interface to the database.

Choosing a Data Management System

The process of selecting an AMS involves specific phases, each with different tasks and milestones. The following resources can help you in the selection process.

- ASAE Information Central (www.asaenet.org/research/).
  Information Central is an information clearinghouse that features a searchable database of literature consisting of more than 5,000 books, articles, and survey data; a compilation of Internet resource links; and other research-oriented information.

- ASAE Listservers. As a member benefit, ASAE provides the opportunity to participate in section listservers. These listservers provide a forum for information exchange on a variety of topics, including AMS vendors and products.

- ASAE Technology Solutions Directory. This directory is available online and in print, usually in the June issue of ASAE's *Association Management*. The directory provides a list of technology-related vendors and consultants along with their products and services. The online version provides links to company Web sites.

- Industry Events. ASAE and other organizations conduct a variety of events addressing various aspects of the AMS selection process. AMS vendors provide product demonstrations periodically.

- Consultants. Reputable consultants have accumulated experience and knowledge from guiding many associations through the process of selecting AMS solutions.

You should use these resources to conduct initial research. The more you know before commencing the selection process, the better equipped your association will be to choose the most appropriate solution.

When choosing a data management system, you may want to consider a team approach, where an overall project leader is appointed, but the evaluation and selection is a collaborative effort. Team members should represent different functional areas of the organization. Although it is not critical for all team members to participate in every aspect of the process (for example, proposal review), there are critical functions that warrant each member's involvement. These include participating in the needs assessment, software demonstrations, debriefings, and team meetings. The team approach offers representation of the association's different needs, varying perspectives when analyzing solutions, and group acceptance of the project as a whole, as well as the selected solution.

Needs Assessment Methodologies

Determining what the association needs is no small task. Whether a consultant is used or the task is managed internally, the most telling information can be obtained via staff interviews. The project leader or consultant should meet with groups representing each functional area of the organization. A functional area may be a crossover of various departments. For example, the meetings area may include participants from the meetings, accounting, and education departments, if individuals from all three departments are involved in meeting planning, management, and registration.

The focus of the interviews should *not* be an in-depth discussion of business processes (unless a complete business process review is desired), but rather an overview of the functional area operations and processes, a review of issues and inefficiencies with current processes and existing systems, and a discussion of requirements. The interviewer should develop a general format for the interview, with relevant topics and questions. Information gathered at this stage forms the basis for the remaining tasks involved in the selection process. It will be used to generate a request for proposal (RFP), develop a product demonstration agenda, and evaluate specific solutions and their ability to fulfill the association's overall requirements.

After the needs assessment, but before releasing an RFP, you may wish to conduct preliminary demonstrations. These demonstrations provide a general, high-level understanding of available AMS products. They are overviews and are not intended to provide in-depth detail; this is reserved for a later stage. Another objective is to begin the solicitation process by determining if the selected vendors should be solicited when it is time to distribute the RFP. Generally, three or four vendors are asked to participate at this stage—those whose products most closely meet the association's needs—and presentations are approximately two hours long.

Preliminary demonstrations often take place after the needs assessment. Once requirements have been established, it is easier to determine the products that most closely meet the association's needs. In some cases, demonstrations can and should take place before the needs assessment. If the organization has never used an integrated AMS or is currently using a very outdated, character-based product, it is helpful to become familiar with the concept of a centralized system and to view available features. This can establish a good foundation as the association begins to assess needs and requirements.

Making Software and Hardware Selections

Vendors are generally solicited with an RFP and are asked to submit a proposal detailing their solutions and associated costs. Information garnered during the needs assessment will be used to develop most of the RFP. Details regarding functional area operations and processes should be outlined, and needs for each functional area should be translated into system requirements or features and should be clearly stated in a format that will allow vendors to indicate their ability or inability to provide required features. It is also helpful to include supporting information (membership applications, conference forms, certification brochures, etc.).

Once the RFP is developed, the team must decide which vendors to solicit. Generally, sending the RFP to a large group of vendors is not recommended. Rather, the association should conduct substantial research beforehand to narrow the vendor pool to four or five suitable vendors. If the association viewed preliminary demonstrations, it will have a select group of potential candidates. Preferably, vendors should have at least three to four weeks to respond, depending on the length of the RFP and the quantity of information requested. The more time they have, the more apt they are to reply with a quality proposal.

Each vendor will submit a proposal, and the level of detail and format will vary. Often, those reviewing proposals will be left with several unanswered questions after the initial review. Those reviewing proposals should note questions as they arise, compile a list for each vendor, and select a medium for addressing the questions. Additionally, a line-item cost comparison should be performed to determine what is included in each proposal. Initial bottom-line costs may vary greatly from vendor to vendor, but once a line-item comparison of all project-related cost components is conducted, the variance may not be as great as it first appears.

Aside from cost, additional criteria for selecting finalists include:

References. Each vendor should be asked to include at least five references. The association should conduct a thorough reference check on all vendors. Develop a list of questions before making the calls; this helps to maintain uniformity. If possible, obtain unofficial references and do a quick check with these as well.

Customization. Those reviewing proposals must analyze the level of customization required to adequately address requirements and understand the vendors' philosophy regarding customization. In a broad sense, there are two types of customizations: those that change the product's source code and those that do not. Some vendors will alter the product's source code and customize the product to meet each association's exact specifications. Others will change the source code only if they are planning to incorporate these changes in the base software. Some vendors will not alter the source code, but rather, will write customizations that do not affect the source code. Before deciding on a vendor, the association should have a clear understanding of these options.

The association should understand that all customizations carry an additional cost over and above the cost of the base software. An alternative to customization is changing organizational business processes to fit the framework of the software as opposed to changing the software to meet association procedures. The association should consider any implications that customization will have on future upgrades. Sometimes, though not always, customizations may not transfer when upgrading. This may result in additional expense.

Support. The organization should thoroughly analyze the vendors' support plans, including methods of support, emergency support, and costs.

Security. The association should give ample consideration to system security and the level of customization the candidate systems provide. One or two staff members who will be maintaining the database should have full access to view and edit all fields. Other staff may need access to write only to those fields that relate specifically to their job, and still others may need only limited viewing rights. Ideally, each person should be given only the amount of access needed to do his or her job, to minimize the risk of inadvertent damage or sabotage of data.

Vendor responsiveness throughout the selection process. If the vendor has been responsive to this point, this may indicate that the company takes customer service seriously. On the other hand, if the vendor has a lackluster attitude, this may indicate the opposite.

Vendor's availability. If timing is critical for the organization and one of the vendors cannot accommodate the association's time line, you may want to eliminate that vendor from further consideration.

Training. Because training is crucial to the association's ability to maximize system performance, training options should be evaluated when making a selection. Return on investment is directly related to the staff's ability to use the system efficiently, and without proper training, this is unlikely. Many undesirable consequences may surface as a result of lack of training (user frustration, incorrect data entry, work-around solutions, and creation of stand-alone databases—all of which defeat the purpose of a centralized database). Although some users may require more training than others, initial training should include all users. A plan for on-going training and new staff training also should be considered.

If your budget is depleted when it's time for training or does not allow for on-going or newcomer training, the association may want to consider a "train-the-trainer" approach to training. This approach involves providing extensive training to select individuals, and in turn, these individuals train other staff. The train-the-trainer method is especially useful for on-going training and new staff training.

Reporting. An association must give due consideration to the reporting capabilities of the candidate systems. An AMS may be easy to use, have fields to store the different kinds of data the association will need, and be developed by a stable, responsive firm, but this is all for naught if the association management can't get the data it needs out of the system quickly, easily, and reliably.

Some systems have a substantial number of built-in or canned reports. But an association will need to report data in ways that fit its culture or that are particular to its needs in mining its unique data set. To that end, there should be some provision for customizing reports that does not wholly rely on the software developer. If an association has to rely entirely on an outside provider to develop customized reports, the cost can easily run to thousands of dollars in the first year, and the association may waste a lot of time waiting for programmers to create reports that fit the association's needs.

As such, there should be a customizable reporting tool built into the system that allows the association to query on fields that may not be a part of the standard, preformatted reports. Otherwise, the application should work well with a third-party reporting tool, such as Crystal Reports, which enables trained users to create ad-hoc reports. Failing that, there may be a person on the association's staff trained in the programming language in which the data tables underlying the user application are written. Finally, a limited number of well-trained association staff may use an all-purpose application, such as Microsoft Access, to query the underlying data tables. Whatever solution is chosen, the ability to get useful data out of the system is critical, and the cost of doing so should be considered as part of the overall direction the association takes in choosing an AMS.

When combined, these criteria should provide a means to select the finalists most suited to the organization.

After narrowing down the vendor pool to two or three (at most) finalists, an in-depth demonstration is the next step. The following guidelines can be used to help reap the greatest benefit from demonstrations.

Script the demonstration. Construct a specific agenda, categorized by functional area. This will allow the association, rather than the vendor, to be in control of the demonstration.

Mandate participation. The project leader must emphasize to staff that the demonstrations must be taken seriously and brief them on evaluation criteria. All participants should attend every demonstration or none at all. Products cannot be evaluated fairly if attendees view only two of three demonstrations.

Schedule demonstrations appropriately. Ideally, demonstrations should be scheduled with no more than one day in between each— otherwise, people tend to forget, making an accurate product assessment and comparison difficult.

Question consistently. The team and other demonstration participants should ask consistent questions of all vendors to obtain a thorough and fair comparison.

Generate a user survey. A user survey can be useful in documenting and assessing participants' reactions to the vendor and product if used correctly and completed fully by all participants for each demonstration.

Conduct a staff debriefing. This meeting should be scheduled shortly, if not immediately, after the final demonstration to solicit attendee feedback and determine the necessary follow-up action.

At this juncture, the association may be ready to make a final decision. However, if there is not a clear level of comfort, the association may want to arrange a hands-on demonstration. This will allow staff members to use the software for specific tasks, serving to truly illustrate navigational aspects, ease of use, and functionality and to possibly eliminate one of the contenders. Remember that users are not yet trained. Core team members may also choose to conduct a site visit to one of the vendors' existing clients and arrange a visit to each vendor's facilities.

After a system has been selected, the association will need to acquire the appropriate hardware. Generally, hardware selections are driven by the selected software. If the association selects a client-server system, a dedicated server will likely be required. Each vendor will be able to provide information regarding product-specific hardware requirements.

Database hosting is an option that is becoming increasingly popular and available. Several AMS vendors have hosting options whereby the system is hosted and managed at the vendor's site or another location determined by the vendor. Data are accessed by the client via secure, fast Internet connections. Benefits of hosting include monthly fees for software and hosting, rather than large initial cash outlays for hardware and software; freedom from finding and retaining qualified staff to manage the database; and remote access to data wherever and whenever needed by staff, regional offices, chapters, members, and any other authorized users.

Data Conversion

Once an AMS has been chosen and a timeline has been set for implementation, the association must focus on data conversion. Data can be converted, archived, or deleted; the association must analyze the data to determine the appropriate option.

- Converting data involves transferring information from the old database(s) into the new database. This will likely include general contact information, recent financial information, and other specific membership information (e.g., join date, membership type).

- Archiving is moving data from the old database to a storage platform that is not immediately accessible from the database. That is, the data are not moved to the new database, but are kept elsewhere on electronic file. Examples of data that may be archived include financial records, events attendance records, and other contact information more than three years old.

- Deleting data is permanently removing data from the old database, neither archiving it nor converting it. Data that can be deleted may include old contact information (e.g., individuals added to the database but with no other activity associated with them), temporary mailing lists, ad hoc committees, and other data with no value.

Prototyping Data

Another consideration is how the converted data appear in the new database. Because of differences between the structure of the old database and the new, the association may have to make some compromises when converting data. Because of these compromises, the association may want to test the data on a prototype system before final implementation. Testing will allow users to see the differences between the two systems and help determine if the new system will support their needs.

The association should consider the time required to convert old data to the new system. A lot of data will have to be "massaged" to convert cleanly into the new system. For example, the old system may have supported a two-digit year for certain date fields ("99" for 1999) while the new system requires a four-digit year ("1999" for 1999). All dates would have to be converted to the four-digit standard before being transferred to the new system. These nuances can take time to address, and the association needs to consider the time needed to convert all critical data to the new system and include this in its system conversion timeline.

An association may choose to run a prototype system to test the data conversion and system operability, running this system in parallel with its existing system. This would require additional work on the part of association staff, including double-keying data (putting the same data into both the old and the new system).

Determining Data Entry Standards

Before determining data entry standards, it is important to consider what condition the original data are in, and how global changes during the conversion process will affect them. This applies not only to the initial effect of the changes, but to more far-reaching consequences. For example, to streamline data entry, a system administrator may change all instances of "P.O. Box" in the database to "PO Box." Then, when the association sends a mailing list to its mail house, the mail house runs the file through a case correction program before printing address labels. The casing process automatically changes all instances of "PO Box" to "Po Box," assuming that "PO" is a word that has inadvertently been double-capitalized, rather than an acronym. Similar problems occur with other acronyms, so it is wise to avoid acronyms altogether in entering data, or else to make certain data are consistently entered in such a way as to obviate the need for case-correction programs.

Equally important in determining data entry standards is consideration of data usage. For instance, an association will often use the data in its database to create a mail-merge letter. It is therefore important to be sure that the data are consistently entered so that they will conform to accepted business standards when they are merged into a letter. For example, some database programs automatically create a salutation field, which concatenates the honorific and last name into a single field, such as "Mr. Smith." This works fine, unless the member gives his or her first name as Pat, Chris, or the like, making it impossible for the person entering the member's record to determine whether to use a masculine or a feminine honorific. In this case, the automatically generated salutation has to be changed manually to the person's first name, so that a mail-merged letter won't begin with the salutation Dear Smith:.

Then, there is the F. Scott problem. If there is no automatically generated salutation field, and the association is in the habit of using a first-name salutation in letters, a member who goes by his or her first initial and middle name is likely to open a letter which begins, Dear F.:. It's not the end of the world, but it certainly destroys the illusion of a personalized letter. In many cases, the solution to this problem is to examine and manually correct the files before merging the letter, but the problem can sometimes be fixed at the data-entry level. In some membership management systems, there is a badge name (or nickname) field, which assumes that the member likes to be called by his or her first name, but can be manually adjusted. Data entry staff should be trained to change the badge name field to the middle name in cases where it is obviously preferred by the member. Then, an association that prefers to address its members by their first name can use the badge name field as the salutation in a merged letter.

The following are some items to consider in determining data entry standards:

- Will members' contact data be used only for printing mailing labels, or will they also be used for field-merged letters? This brings to bear on whether data are entered in all upper-case letters, or in upper and lower case.

- Are most members located in the United States and Canada, or does the design of the database need to accommodate the address and telephone formatting of other countries as well? If membership is at present North American, is there any likelihood that it will expand to other countries?

- Information on members' annual sales or other data that determine dues and fees must be entered uniformly for all members, and in the simplest possible terms, to allow for maximum flexibility in using the data to construct dues matrices and reports.

- If members have multiple company affiliations or multiple addresses, how will these be managed?

- If member demographic information is to be collected, the kinds of data should be determined before setting up demographic tables and should allow for as much flexibility as possible. This way, as the members' needs change, the association can respond to those changes by changing the kind of information it collects. Demographic data collection is expensive and time-consuming, so the association should be as inclusive as its vision allows in designing demographic tables. Is it important to know the educational level of individual members? If an association is fairly broad in the scope of its services, it may want to know the exact job responsibilities and interests of each of its members, in order to target marketing of professional development services. The association may also find this kind of information helpful in refining its focus to better serve the identified interests of its members as their needs evolve.

Once the association has determined how the data will be used, data entry standards must be designed that will facilitate these uses of the data. The key is absolute consistency.

Most associations find that entering the data in upper and lower case is most effective, because it gives maximum flexibility in using the data for mail-merged letters. The U.S. Postal Service prefers all upper case letters on mailing addresses, but it is much easier to convert mixed case letters to upper case than the reverse. Letters written or headed in all caps are generally considered difficult to read and are less-than-standard in common business usage.

The use of abbreviations should be standardized and adhered to. Again, the U.S. Postal Service prefers standard abbreviations without punctuation for addresses; however, many associations eschew abbreviations in letter headings for a more formal appearance. It matters little which way an association decides on this issue, as long as it is consistent throughout its data entry practices. Although this kind of inconsistency may not be obvious on a single envelope, it would be glaring in a printed directory or meeting attendance roster, where "St." may be in the entry just above "Street," and "Blvd." may appear next to "Boulevard." The overall effect would appear sloppy and unprofessional.

With regard to titles, abbreviations are often unavoidable. A member's job title may be too long to fit on one line of an address label unless it is abbreviated. A good source of standard business abbreviations for use in titles is *Postal Addressing Standards,* available at no cost from the U.S. Postal Service (Publication 28, 1–800–238–3150).

Because there is little standardization of job titles, even within a given industry, many association database systems contain a separate field for role. This can be an effective tool for selecting records, if it is applied consistently, because the role field can be constrained to allow only predetermined values. When the number of available values in a field is limited, it is more efficient to query that field for a particular set of records.

Some associations use the role field to indicate an individual's administrative level within his or her organization, such as manager, director, president, and the like. Other associations may use this field to indicate the person's area of expertise, such as human resources, administration, and so forth. These roles can then be used in a query of the database to select multiple records of a particular type, if they are used consistently and kept fairly general. Some associations find it helpful to assign multiple roles to a given member, in an effort to identify more precisely the person's interests.

Communicating Data Entry Standards

Data entry standards should be effectively communicated. All staff and volunteers who will have "write access" (meaning permission to make changes to data) to the system should be thoroughly trained and must understand the importance of consistency in entering data. After initial training, association management should monitor the production of individual staff members and retrain when necessary, to ensure adherence to the standards.

An association should publish and maintain a data entry standards document that is readily accessible to all staff. This document should outline casing standards, when abbreviations are acceptable, what abbreviations are not acceptable, and how titles and roles should be entered into the system. It should specify the minimum required fields for creating a new individual or company record. New employees whose jobs will require them to enter data into the system should be thoroughly trained in its use, with particular attention to the data entry standards document.

If an association is considering migrating its existing database into a new system, the existing data entry standards document should be carefully revised to reflect any change in policy that may be required to accommodate the new software or any anticipated changes in use of the data. In the rare instances where data entry standards must be changed for an existing database system, all employees should be made aware of the change.

General Data Entry Training

There are two levels of training necessary for data entry. Most important is the training of staff whose jobs require them to enter data into the membership system. The second is the basic level of instruction offered for members who may be able to revise their contact information through the association's Web site.

Most database system developers offer generic material for use in training users on the system. This can be helpful in training managers and other first-generation users on a database system. Once the system is populated with an association's own data, however, most associations find it more effective to develop their own training materials. This makes it easier for the new employee to become familiar with the kinds of data he or she will be working with and the kinds of questions that will come up in using the database. Using the association's own data, preferably in a duplicate, training, or test database, it is possible to give employees real-time, true-to-life situations that are likely to arise in entering data, and they can be trained to make appropriate decisions as to how the data should be treated. This training should be as realistic as possible and should cover many of the situations the employee is likely to encounter when normally using the system.

Another important training issue for database users is effective search techniques. There is no way to ensure that no duplicate records are created in the database. An employee may be searching the system for a member who identifies herself as "Peggy Smith," for instance. It may not occur to the employee that the member's name is in the system as "Margaret Smith," and a new duplicate record is created as a matter of course.

Scrupulously monitoring the work of new employees, as well as occasionally checking the work of longer-term employees, is as important as initial training. Many modern membership systems are searchable for records entered by a particular employee, within a given date range. Running a report like this for new employees allows you to scan their work for errors and adherence to data entry standards. It may be a good idea to similarly monitor the work of veteran employees, as well, if less frequently. This process of monitoring allows the system manager the opportunity to retrain employees in the use of the system when necessary or alerts supervisors to the need for employee counseling.

Some membership database systems allow members to edit their own contact or affiliation information from the association's Web site. This can be a great opportunity to cut some data entry costs and get members more involved in taking responsibility for their own information, but it can carry pitfalls of its own.

Members cannot be expected to know the intricacies of data entry standards. Members generally won't care whether their street address is abbreviated, or whether their e-mail address is entered in upper case, lower case, or a mix. They may feel perfectly comfortable using their company's acronym or other trade name—rather than the legal name that is in the database.

There can be some minimal instruction as to what kind of information is expected of a member in updating his or her record, but responsibility for monitoring the data entry rests with the staff entrusted with managing the database. In designing a system that allows members to update their own contact information, there must be an opportunity for that new information to pass by a data entry clerk for approval and editing.

Data Collection

Collecting new data on current and potential members should be aggressive and relentless.

Existing members' records need to be updated regularly, due to an organization's move from one location to another, area code changes, reorganizations, and staffing changes. Members may or may not volunteer this information. The database manager needs to seek out this information by soliciting, at least annually, updated records of members. In associations with institutional membership, this may involve the relatively easy task of sending a list of the organization's affiliated members to a designated primary contact and asking that contact to make any necessary changes. This is more complicated in individual membership associations, because when a member leaves his or her company, the association often loses the only address it has for the member. For this reason, many individual membership associations collect their members' home addresses.

Collecting demographic information on members has become increasingly important. This may involve age, education, seniority, or level of expertise of the individual, or it may involve the specific areas addressed in the person's work. This is particularly important in associations with a relatively broad scope of services, because it enables the association to tailor its professional development and publications marketing strategies to individuals with demonstrated interest in a particular field.

A good example of this is a 1999 survey conducted by the National Association of College and University Business Officers (NACUBO). NACUBO offers a broad range of professional development programs and publications in higher education management. Rather than intensively marketing all its programs and publications to its entire membership, NACUBO identified the job responsibilities and related interests of as many individual members as possible and held down the cost of marketing individual programs.

NACUBO developed a list of twenty-two broad areas in college and university management and subdivided each into specific items to design its survey. The responses were tabulated and recorded in each member's demographic record in specific fields that can be queried in marketing programs and publications related to that field. Thus, materials advertising an accounting workshop can be directed only to persons who have indicated an interest in that subject, and that workshop may be more intensively marketed to individuals who have indicated that they work directly in the field of accounting.

Collecting and recording this kind of data may seem like a daunting task, but technology can greatly reduce the cost of the process. In the NACUBO survey, the survey instrument was developed as a two-page form that could be scanned, and responses were recorded by members darkening circles next to the items in which they had either an interest or a responsibility. The forms were then scanned, and the results, linked to the member's system identification number, were exported to a table, which could then be uploaded directly to the association's database.

Some associations purchase the software and hardware necessary to conduct this kind of survey in-house. Most systems sophisticated enough to do elaborate surveys also require substantial training, as well as a staff person whose job is largely dedicated to the task of developing the surveys and designing the process for uploading each survey to the database. NACUBO decided it made more sense to outsource the design of the survey instrument and the upload process. After the initial, very large mailing of the survey instrument, NACUBO handles ongoing data collection in-house.

In surveying its members, an association must have clear objectives at the outset: What data do we need to collect? What are the data going to be used for? How are we going to transfer the data to the database in a way that allows them to be mined effectively? It is important that the data be formatted in specific, measurable values, in order to benefit from the ability to enter the data in the system economically and to query the data effectively. Trying to save money by creating a survey that is not scannable often backfires when the association has to retain and train temporary employees to manually enter data.

As important as designing a member survey is getting members to fill it out and return it. The design should be colorful and should use a lot of white space, so the survey won't look too complicated to the respondent. Let potential respondents know that the survey is on the way, that it is easy to fill out, and that there is value to them in returning the survey. If a member is expecting a survey, it is likely to trigger a spark of recognition and curiosity, which translates to a greater response rate. A survey that just appears in a member's mailbox and looks daunting to fill out will be treated more as an annoyance and put aside or immediately thrown away. An association might offer a prize drawing, such as a free registration or hotel stay at its annual convention, in which respondents to the survey will automatically be entered. These kinds of prizes can be offered at little or no cost to the association, but add significant value to the respondent.

Response rate in a survey should be viewed in terms of its ultimate value to the association. An initial response rate of 20 percent may seem low, but all the respondents are qualified targets for marketing efforts: they have actually indicated an interest in the product being offered. Additionally, the association will find, over time, that repeated efforts to collect data will yield greater success than initial saturation.

Staffing for Effective Database Management

There are no absolute guidelines as to how many employees are needed to effectively manage an association database. What is important is that the association assigns ownership of the database system to the employee who is responsible for it. In most associations, management of the database falls naturally to the membership department, but in many cases it is a shared function.

Having one employee who is responsible for overseeing all aspects of managing the database goes a long way toward ensuring the integrity of the data it holds. These functions include managing data input, thoroughly training both permanent and temporary employees, assigning security levels to individual employees, and serving as a primary resource for managing and collecting new types of data. That person may or may not have the technical expertise to tinker with the back end of the database, but should have a thorough understanding of its workings, its importance to the association, the effective use of policy to manage data collection and entry, and the ability to communicate these concepts effectively to other staff.

There should also be a technical person working with the database who is thoroughly conversant with SQL (Structured Query Language, pronounced "sequel"), Oracle, UNIX, or whatever programming language regulates the underlying structure of the database. This person may be the same as the database manager, or in a larger association, it may be an employee from the information services department.

Finally, there should be employees who do the actual data entry. There should be enough employees to ensure that data changes are entered in the system in a timely manner. They may be part of the membership department or spread over several different departments, but they must all be thoroughly trained by the database manager, and their work should be regularly monitored.

Managing security levels among staff and volunteers who have access to the association's database is one of the more difficult issues a database manager faces. In some associations, many or all staff members have "read access" to the system, which allows them to look up individual records or query for groups of records. Before gaining "write access" to the database, an employee must be thoroughly trained in all aspects of data entry and, thereafter, should be continuously reminded of the association's data entry standards. Even so, not all employees would have either read or write access to members' financial records stored on the system. This information should be limited to those with a need to know. The ability to void or change invoices might be limited to only those individuals in the association's accounting department. The availability of security levels that would grant access to only those parts of the database that an employee needs to do his or her job is an important factor in choosing a database system. Assuming that security levels are available, they should be scrupulously monitored by the database manager who assigns them.

Many associations grant volunteers read access to parts of the database; some grant write access to volunteers. There are several factors to consider in allowing access to members who do not work directly for the association. First, all employees and volunteers should be asked to sign a confidentiality agreement stating that they will not rent, sell, or otherwise divulge information in the database to outside parties. If an association also grants volunteers write access to the system, it should be aware that volunteers may not be entirely rigorous in adhering to data entry standards, and the association does not have the same leverage in these cases as with employees. The only recourse an association has with a volunteer who fails to meet standards is to monitor and correct all of his or her data entry, or revoke access and risk losing an otherwise valuable asset. Most associations steer around this thorny issue by instituting a policy of read-only access for volunteers.

Putting the Data to Work

While most associations spend a lot of time, money, and energy on selecting and implementing an association management system, the process of using the data collected in the association database is often overlooked. From number of members, to publication orders, to meeting registrations, to certification, associations collect large amounts of data that may help them to better market their products and services. Although some of these data are easily extracted and analyzed, other data require deeper thought and consideration.

Current Membership Numbers and Revenue

Assuming the association is keeping track of its members in the database, and assuming that data are up-to-date and accurate, association executives have immediate access to two key measurements: total members and total membership revenue. Depending on the type of association, this benchmark may occur as infrequently as annually or as frequently as monthly or weekly. Whether the association is a trade, professional, or philanthropic organization, it can track its progress with periodic benchmarking of these two numbers. The association's growth can be measured in terms of current membership compared with one week, one month, one year, or five years ago (or whatever is appropriate), as well as total membership dues revenue measured against the same time period.

There are other statistics that are also easily accessible from the database, provided records have been kept accurately for some period of time. These include:

- membership retention
- market penetration
- lifetime value (LTV)

Membership retention is a relatively easy formula that requires only three numbers: the number of members from some date in the past, the number of new members added since that time, and the total number of members now. One simply subtracts the number of new members from the current members, and divides that number from the number of members in the past. For example:

> On 1/1/1999, XYZ Association had 575 members. On 1/1/2000, XYZ had 612 members, 77 of them being new members. Thus, (612 - 77)/575 = 0.930 or 93% retention.

Retention is an important number, because it tells the association if it's keeping members that it is acquiring or if it is losing an unusually large number of members. Retention is also key because research has shown that acquiring new members and customers can cost anywhere from 8 to 16 times the cost of retaining an existing member or customer.

Market penetration is another relatively easy formula, assuming the association has two key numbers: current number of members and the universe of potential members. For many associations, determining the universe of members can be difficult, especially if the association has a broad range of membership categories. But assuming a universe can be identified, the formula is simple: number of current members divided by the number of the universe. For example:

> On 1/1/2000, XYZ Association, representing accredited higher education institutions in the United States, has 2512 members. The universe of accredited higher education institutions in the United States is 3215. Thus, 2512 / 3215 = .781 or 78%. XYZ Association has a market penetration of 78%.

Market penetration can be important for several reasons. If the association lobbies on behalf of the industry, with higher market penetration it can claim to be "the voice of the industry." High market penetration also increases the value of advertising space in the association's publications. Market penetration also demonstrates growth potential for the association in terms of membership numbers and revenue. High market penetration (over 90%) may not allow for much future growth in terms of member numbers and dues revenue; thus the association may need to look beyond membership dues for additional revenue. On the other hand, low market penetration may be an opportunity for increased dues revenue or may indicate the association is not providing enough value to the market it is serving.

A third statistic that can be mined from the database is LTV. Simply defined, LTV is the total dollar value of a member for the life of his or her membership. That is, if the association adds all revenue received from a member (dues, products, and services) over the entire period of time the member is involved with the association, this is the LTV of the member. Association executives should calculate LTV for their membership to measure whether their recruitment and retention efforts are effective. The key statistics to calculating LTV are average number of years a member stays with the association and the average amount of money (including dues) spent by a member each year.

Multiplying these two numbers together provides the LTV. For example:

> At the XYZ Association, the average member stays in the association for 11 years. The average member spends $2,150 per year with the association, including dues, meeting attendance, and publication purchases. Thus, the LTV of the average member is 11 × $2,150 or $23,650. This is important because while dues for a new member may be only $1,500, the association may choose to spend several multiples of $1,500 to acquire a new member, because the LTV is much higher than one year's dues.

Data Interpretation— What Are the Statistics Saying?

All of these data can be important to the management of the association, especially in identifying trends in membership. Tracking total membership and revenue over the course of several years can demonstrate whether there is a shift occurring in the industry or universe being served by the association. In addition to membership numbers and dues revenue, an association might track data such as purchasing history by company, attendance at association meetings, advertising and sponsorship revenue, and other revenue sources. Tracking these data over time and comparing numbers from year to year can provide associations with great insight into the behavior of their members.

Case Study: The Food and Drug Law Institute

In the mid-1990s, like many other associations representing the food, drug, and medical device industries, the Food and Drug Law Institute (FDLI) was faced with a declining number of top-tier member companies, as a result of corporate mergers. Faced with declining membership numbers and a corresponding decline in membership dues revenue, FDLI looked to its data to determine if a dues increase for the top-tier member companies was warranted. An analysis of the data showed that while the average company was sending about 2 people per year to FDLI educational events, the largest companies were sending more than 10. Through greater participation, the top-tier companies were getting a greater benefit from membership, along with a greater amount of discounts compared to the nonmember price. Thus FDLI's board agreed to raise dues on this membership segment to balance the amount of benefit to the company against the amount of dues being paid and to offset the loss of revenue due to mergers among the largest companies. The end result was that 100 percent of FDLI's top-tier companies maintained their membership, even with a 50 percent increase in annual dues.

Using the Database for Recruitment, Retention, and Marketing

Marketing

Perhaps the greatest value of the association's database is the marketing data collected. Associations can use their data to help them market products and services more effectively and identify growth areas, new products, and maturing or dying products.

Using Recency/Frequency/Monetary Value (RFM) analysis, the association can mine its data for information on its best members or customers. Simply put, RFM suggests that the best customers in the database are those who have recently purchased a product or service, have purchased several products and/or services, and have spent greater sums of money on these products and services. With a well-maintained database, the association can analyze the buying habits of its members and customers and develop a target list of those members and customers most likely to purchase another product or service from the association.

In addition to RFM, the association's data can also help identify growth areas, new products, and maturing or dying products. This information is gleaned from sales data but will require creative thinking and analysis on the part of association staff. To identify growth areas and new products, staff must analyze the trends in the types of products and services being purchased. Do the products and services with greater sales have a common theme among them? For example, if a printed piece on a particular subject is selling well, is there an opportunity to develop a seminar or educational session around the topic? Could complementary software be created?

Is there a particular format that sells better than others? Do the members and customers prefer electronic formats to printed material? Do they prefer video-conferencing to on-site meetings? All of this information can be gleaned from a thoughtful analysis of existing data.

Finally, sales data can provide insight into products and services whose appeal is waning. Analyzing the sales trends of a particular product may show that sales are decreasing. Before concluding that the product has matured, association staff must weigh other factors, including quantity and quality of marketing for the product, timeliness of the issue addressed by the product, and other issues, such as pricing. Keeping in mind all these considerations, sales trends can help association staffers decide if further efforts should be made on maturing or dying products.

Retention

Retaining members is a continuous challenge for all associations. Communicating clearly and appropriately with members can be key to retention. Besides telling staff how many current members there are, the association database can track how often members are "touched" throughout the year. Association staff should record each contact made to members, be it through direct mail promotion of a product or service, notices about upcoming business meetings, or e-mail announcements about legislative issues. Each time the association speaks to its members, the database can track what was said and when it was said. These data can be used to ensure that members are being communicated with in a timely and appropriate manner.

In addition to tracking how and when the association is communicating with members, the database can also provide clues as to when a member is most likely to drop membership. If the association has been tracking join dates and drop dates for an extended period, these data can tell the association at what point in a member's "life" he or she is most likely to drop membership and provide the association an opportunity to address the issue before the member drops.

For example, by analyzing the join and drop dates of its members over the past 5 years, the XYZ Association found that the average member drops in his or her seventh year of membership. Armed with these data, XYZ Association created a special program where all members entering their seventh year of membership were personally contacted by a member of the association's board of directors, to ensure members' needs were being addressed.

Recruitment

Associations can use their data to develop a profile of the "perfect" member. By collecting a variety of demographic data, the association can determine what the most profitable member "looks like" and then target nonmembers who look like the perfect member.

Depending on the type of association, demographics for trade associations could include company size (sales and staffing), industry served, and geographic location. For professional societies, demographics might include profession, experience, level of education, age, gender, geographic location, household income, and more. The types of demographic criteria to consider are limited only by your imagination.

In addition to the "perfect" member, associations can also use the data to identify nonmembers who purchase a lot of products and services and approach them about membership.

Tracking

Like all other promotions, membership promotion is a sales cycle. Thus the cycle and the promotion efforts can be tracked through the use of source codes, which are recorded in the association database for effectiveness.

For example, the XYZ Association, a professional society, does a direct mail promotion to 10,000 potential members. A source code is printed on the reply form, so when a new member joins from that form, the source code is recorded in the database, showing from which promotion the new member was acquired. In addition to the response form, the letter that is part of the direct mail solicitation lists a special department number with the phone number so that the source code is tracked in the database when a new member calls to join. By vigilantly tracking the source of all new members, the XYZ Association is able to identify which membership promotions are effective and which are not.

Conclusion

As this chapter demonstrates, the process of choosing, implementing, and managing an AMS is not to be taken lightly. Nor is it a process that ends with the installation of a new piece of software. Effective management of the AMS is achieved only through vigilant attention to the details of the database and the use of the data.

REFERENCES

American Society of Association Executives. *Association Technology Trends 1997,* Washington, D.C.: American Society of Association Executives, 1997.

Technology Solutions Directory. *Association Management* Vol. 51 No. 6 (June 1999): T1–T50.

Wes Trochlil is president of Effective Database Management (EDM) in Fairfax, Va. Trochlil is an independent consultant providing associations with a variety of services for association management systems, including selection, implementation, project management, documentation, and training. Before founding EDM, he was vice president of McKinley Marketing, Inc., a consulting firm that provides affinity marketing programs to associations. Trochlil has nearly ten years of association management experience and has served as director of membership, marketing, and customer service for the National Association of College and University Business Officers, the Food and Drug Law Institute, and the Food Processing Machinery & Supplies Association. He is a frequent writer and speaker for the American Society of Association Executives (ASAE), the Greater Washington Society of Association Executives (GWSAE), and the Canadian Society of Association Executives (CSAE).

An alumnus of the University of Tennessee at Knoxville, **Michael Connor** had a long and sordid career in the food and beverage industry, including two years as Maitre d' at the renowned Restaurant Nora in Washington, D.C. He then spent five years as a catering and convention services manager with Hyatt Corporation, eventually transitioning into data management and training with Hyatt's massive client database. When he heard the National Association of College and University Business Officers (NACUBO) was looking for a "computer geek with a strong customer service background," Connor heeded the call. At NACUBO, he manages the membership database, publication of the membership directory, and employee training; he's currently coordinating the migration of their membership database to the Web.

Loretta M. DeLuca is the founder and president of DelCor Technology Solutions, Inc., an independent technology management consulting and systems integration firm located in Silver Spring, Md. DeLuca has more than 16 years of experience as an information technology consultant to the association and nonprofit community and is currently an active consultant. Throughout the years, she has accumulated a wealth of knowledge regarding the internal workings of nonprofit organizations and in the systems and applications available to fulfill their unique requirements. DeLuca is a member of the American Society of Association Executives (ASAE) and holds a seat on ASAE's Technology Section Council. She is also a member of the Greater Washington Society of Association Executives (GWSAE) and a frequent presenter at ASAE conferences and Knowledge Networks.

CHAPTER FIVE

Budget Theory and Practice: How to Make Numbers Add Up to Your Success

Stephen M. Lewis

IN ALL WORK ENVIRONMENTS, nothing is more feared and respected than a good budget. Budgets can range from bad guesses to well-reasoned and accurate estimates. They can mean the difference between project failure and approval, and between staff demotion and promotion. Whether you hate them or love them, budgets are critical to the success of any nonprofit or for-profit entity.

Using financial and other numbers to set and track success can seem daunting. However, you can use numbers to guide decision making, strategy development, program implementation, tracking, and reporting. Good budget practices and theories allow you to turn simple numbers into useful data, information, and finally, knowledge. This chapter addresses the successful development and dissemination of valuable budgetary data, information, and knowledge for both internal and external decision makers.

Data: The Right Path

The road to success is paved with good retention and recruitment data. Many organizations track overall retention rates, but they seldom separate that information by membership category or use it when developing lifetime value estimates. Recruitment data are critical to building a sustainable, well-funded membership growth program. By learning how to collect and track retention and recruitment data, you build a solid foundation for membership success.

Unless your database includes an automatic membership retention rate tracking function, you probably collect these data manually. Many associations take an electronic "snapshot" of their full membership each year. By comparing a list of all members in, say, December 1998 to all members in December 1999, an association can determine how many 1998 members opted not to renew in 1999. By dividing the number of nonrenewed members by the total 1998 membership, an overall attrition and retention rate can be determined.

For example, ABC Association has 10,000 members at the end of 1998. Of that number, 1,500 decide not to renew in 1999. By dividing the nonrenewing group number by the total 1998 membership, you know that ABC's attrition rate was 15 percent, and its retention was 85 percent.

Many associations also track retention rates for each membership category. For example, by knowing that individual membership retention numbers are lower than corporate membership retention, an association executive can turn these simple data into useful decision-making information. When resources are scarce, it makes good sense to spend every membership dollar on the most appropriate membership segment.

Recruitment data also can improve decision making. The American Water Works Association (AWWA) in Denver uses a simple Direct Mail Cost Justification spreadsheet (see p. 81) to analyze all its mailed membership recruitment campaigns. AWWA estimates and tracks the following data:

- hard costs spent per member recruited (development, printing, mail house, postage, and so forth)
- hard costs the association is willing to bear to recruit each member
- response rates on the promotion

AWWA enters estimates on development and distribution costs for the direct mail piece, along with expected or "bearable" recruitment cost estimates, then decides whether to conduct the mailing. If it decides to proceed, it tracks actual recruitment results via a source code on all applications for that mailing. AWWA can then determine its expenses and income on each direct mail effort.

Recruitment and retention data can help you budget for any membership campaign. Whether you are considering launching member-get-a-member campaigns, exhibiting at trade shows, advertising, initiating direct sales, or other efforts, the bottom line comes down to dollars spent versus dollars and value returned to the association.

Each association has a unique set of parameters for determining how much it will budget to recruit or retain a particular member. Some associations, including lobbying groups, subsidize or virtually "give away" their membership to dramatically expand their roles and their influence with legislators and regulators. Other associations run membership as a typical for-profit business, providing a product (membership) at a cost that is somewhat higher than developing and delivering that product.

How does your association approach membership budgeting? Is membership a profit center? If so, your goal is to develop budgets that maximize return on investment. Is membership subsidized to provide value to the association in other ways, such as lobbying clout? If so, your budget may focus on recruiting and retaining a high volume of members, as opposed to very targeted groups of deeply involved members.

A membership budget is a business plan. It shows where you will spend money and how much you will spend and estimates the returns you expect on your investment. Membership budgets should include (but are not limited to) the following expense and income items.

Membership Expense Data Checklist

- *Recruitment costs.* In addition to paying staff salaries and overhead, association recruitment costs should cover the conceptualization, design, development (e.g., printing), and delivery (e.g., mail house and postage) costs for all staff-initiated recruitment programs. Think about all your efforts, including direct mail, advertising, telemarketing, exhibiting, and direct sales. Detail how many of these programs you plan on administering. Whether you are a new or seasoned budget developer, you may want to work with local service providers to specify and estimate various costs to develop and implement programs in the budget year ahead. Some costs, such as the cost of paper for printing brochures and applications, may change substantially from year to year.

- *Member-to-member recruitment costs.* If you have a member-get-a-member campaign, you will need to set forth the cost of developing the campaign, distributing education materials, and coordinating any member recruiter gift program (including gift costs).

- *Retention programs.* As with recruiting efforts, consider all aspects of staff- and volunteer-initiated retention programs. Set forth a specific schedule of retention efforts, from initial dues invoice or reminder to your last effort to keep a member on your roles. Estimate the average percentage of members who will receive each of these retention messages or packages and develop a cost to administer each program. If you work with regional offices or sections, consider possible costs to coordinate your efforts with these affiliates.

- *Travel.* Although travel directly related to recruiting and retention should be set forth under those program areas, you may want to include in your budget estimated costs to travel to other associations in your field and to other educational events that will improve your contacts and ability to succeed. Be sure to include airfare, ground transportation, room, and board in your estimates.

- *Subscriptions/memberships.* Include costs to subscribe to educational publications or professional societies.

- *Supplies.* If you are responsible for collecting your own office supplies and member-related items, such as membership lapel pins or customer giveaways, specify your supply needs in this area of the budget.

- *Complimentary materials.* The link between membership satisfaction and customer service often requires a budget for "make-good" items, such as complimentary member publications and products.

• *Membership committee costs.* If you are responsible for working with
an association membership committee, you may need to develop
estimates for member and staff travel to committee meetings, meeting
room and meal or entertainment expenses, facilitation costs, conference calls, and other related committee support or communication
costs.

Membership Income Data Checklist

• *Membership dues income.* Identifying the sources of your membership
income will help you make management decisions regarding recruiting and retention. Some associations use a simple spreadsheet that
shows the different member categories, the anticipated number of
members in each category, their corresponding dues amounts, and a
total amount of anticipated dues income for these categories. Other
associations, especially ones with anniversary-year memberships that
allow members to receive benefits for twelve months after their sign-
up date, use accrual accounting spreadsheets. These spreadsheets calculate the monthly income received from members each year. For
example, a member joining from June of one year until June of the
next would represent only seven months of income (June through
December) of the current calendar year. So, accrual spreadsheets need
to show the actual amount of dues dollars realized by the association.
These figures range from one-twelfth to the full dues amount for the
year. Regardless of how your association tracks dues income, your
budget will need to include this key figure. Develop a spreadsheet
that breaks out the number of members in each category and the
corresponding dues amounts, then enter estimates of future growth
or automatically calculate what would happen to your dues income
if you saw regular membership dues or roll changes over the years.
In addition, you will be able to see where you need to concentrate
recruiting and retention efforts, to obtain the best results.

• *Affinity programs.* Although affinity programs, such as car rental discounts, insurance, affinity credit cards, and other programs, are not
strictly related to "membership" income, virtually all of them stem

from your membership efforts. If you are responsible for implementing group buying and other affinity programs for members, you should track estimated income from these areas. First, you need to estimate the level of member involvement or program usage. You may want to discuss average adoption rates with suppliers who are providing these services or contact colleagues who can help set your expectations. Once you know your participation estimate, multiply it by the average amount of expected income for each program to determine overall income. Once you have a goal set for involvement, you can determine how much staff time or other association expenses will be needed for success.

The specific retention, recruitment, and related expense or income data for your budget will vary, depending on your association's goals and tracking systems. Identifying essential data sets, as in the case study below, will ensure that you turn simple numbers into usable information.

Information: Turning Data into Action

When you compile data into something more valuable than just a bunch of numbers, you are developing actionable information. You should compile both *hard* and *soft* costs. Hard costs are those black-and-white expenses directly related to a specific project, such as printing or postage in a direct mail campaign. Soft costs include project administration or oversight, especially in associations that do not require employees to track actual time spent on specific projects. A good example of hard-cost tracking is seen in the case study example which follows.

Case Study:
AWWA Membership Direct Mail Cost Justification

Target:
2,138 nonmembers

Categories	Totals	Cost per thousand
Letter printing (.028 each)	$59.86	$28.00
Application coding (.011 each)	$23.52	$11.00
#10 envelopes	$59.80	$27.97
#9 envelopes	$37.95	$17.75
Filework/lettershop	$1,200.00	$561.27
List costs	$726.72	$339.91
Postage	$213.80	$100.00
SUBTOTAL	**$2,321.65**	**$1,085.90**

Bearable recruiting costs	$135.00
% Response needed	0.80 %

Total members recruited	50
Actual response rate	2.34 %

Subtotal income	$6,750.00
Total direct costs	$2,321.65

NET INCOME	**$4,428.35**
LIFETIME VALUE	**$68,650.00***

* LTV calculation is based on the average number of years of membership in this category, multiplied by annual dues, conference attendance, and publication purchases (not adjusted for inflation).

Measuring hard costs and return rates will help you to accurately determine where to apply resources, take risks, and guide recruitment and retention dollars. Most association leaders rightly believe that substantial resources should be spent on retaining current members because it is usually easier to retain an existing member than to recruit a new one. By compiling member retention data at one Virginia-based association, however, a membership director learned that organization membership retention stood at 99 percent. Instead of spending 65 percent of her membership budget on retention, she was able to reallocate her resources to bring in more new members, while keeping retention at existing levels.

Compiling information on soft costs also improves success. For the overall association, soft costs include the cost to maintain your building, cost of employee health and other benefits, and cost of the general overhead of running an association. Membership soft costs can be found on both the expense and income sides of the equation.

Your association's overall membership expenses include the dollars it takes to provide services to members. Although membership employees may be involved in marketing recruitment and retention programs, other employees may be devoted to developing member benefits, from newsletters to training programs to lobbying efforts. If possible, membership managers should consider the costs of developing and delivering member benefits when compiling a budget. You may find that your association is spending $1,000 to service a $150 membership.

Soft-cost information is useful in day-to-day recruiting and retention activities, such as development of direct mail collateral material. Explaining an association's membership value or true cost to provide service to prospects can convince them to make the "buy" decision. In addition, soft-cost information can help guide strategic initiatives, from membership planning to restructuring.

The cost to provide service to an average member can be calculated by analyzing estimates of the following:

- number of employees devoted to delivering member benefits, including education
- number of employees involved in retention—member education, networking, marketing, etc.

- average percentage of time or total salary required to deliver member benefits or retention programs
- overhead (percentage of building, human resources, and other administrative costs required)
- information technology costs (usually in overhead and usually a large cost)

Cost to provide service will vary, depending on membership categories. For example, an association may not directly provide service to individual members with its government affairs or lobbying program. If corporate members stand to gain the most from government affairs programs, the cost to service them should be higher than the cost to service individuals. In any case, every association program that provides a service to a segment of membership should be incorporated into soft-cost calculations.

Value usually differs from cost—both hard and soft—based on perspective. Cost is determined by those providing services, while value is determined by those receiving services. Although staff members can readily calculate how much the association spends to deliver services, members are the best judges of what those services are "worth" in the marketplace.

Some associations periodically survey members in different categories to determine what value they place on different benefits. The surveys usually ask questions such as, "How much would you expect to spend on a service such as _____ (e.g., government affairs, an industry newsletter, or educational event) if you or your organization had to develop or collect this information alone?" In short, smart association executives solicit members for critical information about the value provided by the association. If potential or existing members question the valuation numbers, they can be informed that their peers developed the estimates.

One New York-based association includes the following hard-cost and member-value information in its membership benefits valuation:

- cost for membership subscriptions and publications
- cost for local section/affiliate newsletters
- employment advertisements (based on average use)

- discounts on publications, seminars, and conferences (based on average use)
- regulatory alerts (based on member value)
- government affairs assistance (based on member value)
- public affairs assistance—media placement/industry image building (based on member value)
- hotline assistance (based on average use multiplied by average hourly consulting costs)

In addition to determining soft expense figures, budgeters should analyze the value or income that is indirectly tied to membership. For example, many associations track the number of member versus non-member purchases, from conference attendance to purchases of association products. This information can help a budgeter determine which membership types are the best overall association customers or purchasers throughout the "lifetime" of their membership. By knowing a member's lifetime value to the association, the manager can justify different budgets for members with different lifetime values.

Of all the membership value estimates, lifetime value takes the most effort to calculate. True lifetime value can incorporate annual dues (adjusted for inflation), average conference attendance, product purchases, member-get-a-member recruitment efforts, enhancement of association image due to high-profile members, and even the value of sharing volunteer expertise in association product development.

In the direct mail cost justification worksheet (see page 81), AWWA opted to calculate an easily understood version of lifetime value. By knowing its attrition rate for that category of members (12 percent), AWWA divided one member by that rate (1 divided by 0.12) to determine that the average tenure for a member in that category would be 8.33 years. Using simple math, AWWA multiplied average membership tenure by specific annual revenue figures.

Other information variables affecting your ability to turn membership data into action include business rules, such as accrual calculations. Some associations spread out, or accrue, a year's worth of membership dues over twelve months. Others realize the entire dues income in the month it was received at the association. If your success is measured based on monthly accruals or your cash processing staff are not able to handle large volumes of membership transactions, don't conduct the majority of your membership recruitment or retention campaigns at the same time of year.

Turning your association's membership data into actionable information will allow you to develop and justify appropriate income and expense budgets. The next step is sharing this information and spreading the knowledge you have compiled.

Knowledge: Sharing What You Know

Once you have compiled data into useful membership information, you need to make sense and use of that information by sharing your knowledge with volunteers and other association leaders. Numbers often speak volumes in support of your strategic plans; anyone who has witnessed association board members pore over financial spreadsheets can attest to this. Numbers alone can mean just about anything, which is why you need to add your knowledgeable interpretation to budget information to make it valuable.

Making sense of information requires appropriate membership tracking, testing, and reporting programs. The greatest ideas in the world are meaningless until you can prove they were great, based on results. Every membership solicitation, whether for retention or recruitment, should be coded and tracked to determine its actual results. With a good tracking system, you can afford to take risks on new creative approaches, formats, and membership program ideas.

A professional engineering society was able to change its direct mail mix, after testing a letter that involved humor. The society had long used direct mail letters with a business-like tone and pages of information on membership value. Average response rates ranged from 1.2 to 2.5 percent. After testing and tracking a new, three-paragraph letter, which including a cartoon drawing of an egg-head volunteer, the association learned that its members responded to the humorous piece to the tune of a 6.5 percent average response rate.

If your association conducts just a few recruitment or retention campaigns each year, you probably can analyze and make sense of your membership tracking information by reviewing overall results. If you have multiple campaigns, however, you should consider developing a membership sales report. AWWA develops and implements more than 130 annual membership campaigns, including direct mail, advertising, member-get-a-member, and telemarketing. By analyzing information from each of these campaigns in one report, staff members can easily separate the winning programs from the risky ones. The AWWA membership sales report identifies each membership campaign with a different source code—a six-character code unique to the effort. For example, a telemarketing campaign to international prospects conducted in September 2000 might be coded TMI900. Under the code, there is a one-line description of the campaign. Next to the descriptor, a spreadsheet shows the total effort and results (number of calls, direct expenses, number of members recruited) and a percentage rate of return for that particular campaign. With a glance, the membership manager can determine where to allocate or reallocate budgets.

Monthly sales tracking reports also can be used to develop accurate annual budgets and marketing plans. Savvy association professionals often develop compelling reasons to increase membership expense budgets, based on the ratio of membership expenses to dues income. By showing how much membership income is developed with the investment of each membership marketing dollar, association managers can show the need for additional resources. In addition, sales reports accurately predict recruitment and retention results, based on past success. Using a combination of cost-justification spreadsheets and sales reports, membership professionals demonstrate tight budgeting and appropriate risk-taking abilities.

Your ability to present accurate budgetary information determines your business acumen and clout within an organization. When sharing your knowledge with volunteers, consider organizing your presentation along these four lines:

- processes
- deliverables
- results
- plans

First, explain the processes you used to collect, assemble, and analyze data. Discuss how your tracking system was developed and, specifically, what and how it tracks your program success. Unless people are familiar with these systems, your explanation will build your credibility and minimize the number of questions you will face. Imagine the response to a presentation that started with the statement, "Our lifetime value on this recruiting campaign was $63,000!" A little explanation goes a long way.

Second, present all relevant deliverables. You may want to include an explanation or example of your cost-justification sheet, recruitment or retention piece (direct mail, ad, telemarketing script, and so forth), or membership sales report. When possible, include charts showing your successes. Good ideas include return on investment, projected results versus actual results, even a comparison of the total number of membership campaigns last year versus this year. All these items will build your case and allow you to paint a picture as much with numbers as with words.

Show your fellow staff and superiors that you know precisely what you are doing and where you are going with the budget. After you have laid out past successes, share possible strategies for the future, including projected costs and results. With the tracking systems, data, and information on your side, the guesswork is gone. Ideas that previously seemed merely creative or downright risky are now worthy of considerable attention.

Numbers, with analysis, tell a convincing story. By understanding how to collect, track, and turn data into useable reports and synthesis, you enhance your credibility, improve prospects for future membership success, and coach staff on how to make their membership roles more meaningful. In short, budgeting is simple math—an equation that demonstrates the true value you and your program provide to any association.

BIBLIOGRAPHY

Butler, Wilford A., ed. *Attracting, Organizing and Keeping Members.* Washington,
D.C.: American Society of Association Executives, 1989.

Lewis, Stephen M., and Richard P. Whelan. "Lifetime Value: Quantifying the
Value That All Members Bring to Your Association." *Membership
Developments* (December 1999): 1–6.

McInnis, Jan. "Anti-Retention Program Guarantees Attrition." *Membership
Developments* (April 1998): 1–5.

Ross, Debra Lynn. "ENA Reaps 24.8 Percent Membership Growth."
Membership Developments (February 1998): 1–6.

Sirkin, Arlene Farber, and Michael McDermott. *Keeping Members: The Myths and
Realities.* Washington, D.C.: ASAE Foundation, 1995.

Walker, David W. "1998 Keystone Awards for Excellence in Membership."
Membership Developments (September 1999): 1–3.

Stephen M. Lewis is communications & marketing group director for the American Water Works Association (AWWA) in Denver, Colorado. He is responsible for association public affairs, marketing/sales, and membership. In coordination with AWWA's volunteer executive councils and committees, Lewis and his staff manage AWWA programs that account for 75 percent of AWWA's annual revenue.

Formerly, Lewis lobbied for the National Independent Energy Producers in Washington, D.C. He has also served as director of communications for the National Automated Clearing House Association. He began his career as a political columnist for newspapers in Colorado, and he served as press secretary to former U.S. Senator Timothy Wirth.

CHAPTER SIX

Volunteers

Ginger Nichols, CAE

WHO NEEDS VOLUNTEERS? You do, if you want to maximize the effectiveness of your membership program. There are times, however, when every association executive wonders if volunteers are worth the trouble. After all, you have to find them, train them, communicate with them, recognize them, and occasionally finish projects they did not complete, or fix their mistakes. Why bother?

There are three strong reasons to incorporate volunteers into your membership program. First, it helps build organizational strength. That strength comes not only from the stable or growing membership recruited or retained with the help of volunteers, but also from the sense of ownership that volunteers gain when they become active ambassadors and visible advocates for the association.

Second, member volunteers have credibility that paid staff or consultants can never have. They can discuss the association peer-to-peer— as one who experiences its benefits as a fellow member. Moreover, they promote the association because they believe in it. It is a personal choice, not their job. Never underestimate the power of peer-to-peer communication.

Finally, using volunteers extends the membership resources of the association. Volunteers can provide the extra hands that enable an association to do the things that might go by the wayside in the crush of daily business, touches such as personal invitations to prospects and special welcomes to new members. These personal connections forge the ties that foster membership loyalty and association success.

This is not a one-way street. Volunteers gain from their experience, as well. They have a sense of giving back to their profession or industry. Recognition of their work leads to greater prestige among their peers and perhaps even enhanced professional opportunities. Active volunteers gain an insider's knowledge of the organization and enhance the value of their membership. They may learn new skills or acquire new knowledge that helps them advance professionally or personally. They also make new friendships and enlarge their network of colleagues.

Much has been written about the special considerations in working with volunteers. Here are five guidelines that association executives should keep in mind for every volunteer placement.

1. *Match the job to the volunteer.* First, evaluate the requirements of the volunteer job to be filled. What skills or special knowledge does it require? How much of a commitment is necessary? What are the benefits to the volunteer? Once these requirements are known, look for members who are a good fit. If members' skills and interests are included in the association's database, the task is much easier. When recruiting volunteers, the most effective pitch is to define why that particular individual is the right one for a specific job.

2. *Clearly define expectations.* It is worthwhile to develop job descriptions for each volunteer position. The job description should spell out the exact duties, the timeframe for their performance, the time commitment required, what training will be provided, who the volunteer reports to, and the financial considerations (expected to pay own travel costs, etc.). As part of or in addition to a job description, a specific committee or volunteer charge is valuable. The charge should describe the expected outcomes and how success is defined. Having all these points in writing helps avoid misunderstandings and gives volunteers clear direction.

3. *Provide appropriate training and information.* Many volunteers fail, or fail to reach their potential, because they do not receive the training and information they need to succeed. Association executives must think carefully about what preparation their volunteers need to achieve their goals. In some cases, it may be as simple as talking points for a telephone call. For more complex tasks, such as recruitment, a formal training session with role playing may be necessary. Always look at the task from the volunteer's perspective and ask: What do I need to know to succeed?

4. *Assure appropriate follow up.* Use deadlines to keep tasks on schedule. Progress reports serve as early warning signs for problems. Make it easy for volunteers to report their results. Keep the dialogue going both ways by checking in with volunteers from time to time.

5. *Thank and recognize volunteers.* Thanks and recognition are essential factors in motivating and retaining volunteers. There has never been a volunteer who has been thanked too often! Look for creative and fun ways to recognize volunteers in many settings. Recognition before their peers can be a powerful tool not only for providing a fulfilling experience for current volunteers but also for recruiting new ones who would like to bask in that limelight. Ribbons are a time-tested means of recognizing volunteers, as well as photos in the association magazine or newsletter. Be creative! Tie colorful streamers that say "thanks" to the stem of their glasses at a meal or reception. Use a balloon bouquet at their luncheon or banquet table. Bring a celebratory cake (or ice cream or pizza) to a committee meeting. Give special little gifts to volunteers at a phone-a-thon. Your thought really counts when thanking and recognizing your volunteers.

Using Volunteers in Your Membership Program

Associations use volunteers in virtually every aspect of their membership programs. The most common volunteer activities fall into three broad categories: planning, recruitment, and retention.

Planning activities

A frequent problem with membership marketing plans is that they are too insular or inwardly focused. Sometimes, plans are just updated mechanically from year to year, without regard to changes in the environment in which the association is operating. Involving volunteers in membership plan development helps prevent these shortcomings by providing a real-world view from the member's perspective. Here are some of the ways to involve volunteers in planning activities:

- *Formulation of planning assumptions.* Certain assumptions are implicit in the development of any marketing plan. Convene volunteers in a brainstorming session to articulate the assumptions that should underlie the membership plan. Participants in such a session should include a broad cross-section of the association's membership to provide the most diverse range of viewpoints and experience. Planning assumptions can address topics such as overall growth or decline of the industry, profession, or interest; impact of mergers and consolidation; new technology or innovation in the field; shifts in revenue or income; or changes that affect who future membership prospects may be. Assumptions generated in brainstorming sessions need to be validated by objective sources to the extent possible so that the plan is not built solely on the opinions of a few members.

- *Competitive analysis.* Volunteers can be invaluable in researching and analyzing the competition your association is facing, both from other membership organizations and for-profit suppliers of products and services. Some associations assign one member of their membership committee to monitor, collect information, and report on each of their competitors.

- *Message creation.* Advertising agencies have long recognized the value of testing their messages in focus groups. Associations can use their volunteers to take advantage of this approach. Note the words volunteers themselves use when discussing your services and benefits. Chances are these are the words that will resonate with your prospective members.

Recruitment of new members

"My members won't recruit," is a lament often heard from association executives, who then abandon any hope of involving volunteers in their recruitment activities. There are, however, other ways volunteers can support membership recruitment, including generating prospects and serving as event hosts.

Prospect generation. Even when members are loath to actually recruit, they will often volunteer to provide names of potential members. This is one of the most effective ways to build a prospect database, because the prospects have been "prequalified" by current members. Supplier members, in particular, may be willing to share names from their customer lists. In addition to contact information, ask volunteers to provide background information, such as areas of particular interest or special skills that will contribute to the prospect's profile. This inside information can be effectively used to tailor a targeted message. Remember to check all member-generated prospect lists against the roster of current members.

Event hosts. Associations that invite nonmembers to attend association meetings can use hosts to welcome these prospects to the event and talk with them about the association. This strategy is even more effective when combined with a follow-up telephone call within the week. Be sure that someone "asks for the order," that is, asks the prospect to join.

Phone calls/personal visits. Short of launching a full-blown member-get-a-member campaign, associations can use volunteers to follow up with prospects who have requested membership information. After all, those who have taken the initiative to ask about membership are the association's hottest prospects. A brief telephone call to be sure the prospect received the information and to respond to questions often provides the impetus for the prospect to act promptly and positively on the decision to join.

Member-Get-a-Member campaigns. More than a third of associations conduct member-get-a-member (MGM) campaigns, according to ASAE's *Policies & Procedures in Association Management* (1996) and often to great success. In structuring the campaign, there are four key considerations from a volunteer standpoint. First is the complexity of the program. Will volunteers simply be asked to provide prospect names? Or, will staff furnish leads and materials, with volunteers expected to make the calls and close the sales? To encourage maximum participation and success, the level of effort must be appropriate for the membership.

Second, carefully plan the level of support that staff can provide to volunteers. Let volunteers know if they should handle correspondence, follow-up telephone calls and generate their own prospects, or if they can get leads of potential members from the office staff. It is essential to provide regular updates to volunteers on the status of their prospects and to let them know right away when one joins or is approved for membership.

Third, consider what types of incentives are appropriate. Associations offer everything from association "dollars" (redeemable for registration fees or association products) to tote bags and coffee mugs to opportunities to win luxurious trips. In some associations, members will not participate without substantial incentives; in others, members are insulted when the organization tries to buy their participation or offers trinkets of little value. Knowing your members is the only path to selecting the appropriate incentives.

Finally, create multiple ways to recognize and thank your volunteers. This is a fundamental component of any volunteer program, but it is especially critical for MGM campaigns that rely substantially on volunteer effort. A letter of thanks from the association president is in order anytime a volunteer recruits a member. Photos and articles in the association publication, recognition at the annual conference, special badge ribbons and invitation-only receptions are just some of the ways that associations reward their volunteers who recruit new members.

Retention activities

Once new members have been recruited, it is critical to make them feel welcome and engage them actively in the association. Volunteers frequently are the linchpins to these retention activities.

Welcome/ambassadors. Calling new members to welcome them to the association is one of the most enjoyable volunteer tasks in any association. Be sure to provide the volunteers with a list of frequently asked questions (and the answers) they might encounter from new members and clear instructions about what to do if they get a question they cannot answer (do not "wing it"; immediately forward it to staff for response). This is a great opportunity to ask a new member why they joined, what they hope to get from their association membership, and their special areas of interest. Collecting this information on a response form allows staff to enter it into the database and use it for marketing and for involving new members in association activities. New member calls are excellent opportunities to involve volunteers who cannot travel to meetings or have limited time for volunteer activities.

Mentors/buddies. It can be frightening to walk into a room full of strangers. Volunteers can ease this stressful situation by serving as a mentor or buddy to a new member or first-time attendee. This can be as simple as a telephone call before the meeting or conference and an arrangement to meet before the opening session. Be sure the volunteer has complete information about the meeting on hand before the call. This can be an effective way to involve a volunteer on a one-time basis.

Follow up with lapsed members. This is a more difficult, but extremely important, task. It requires substantial preparation both by staff and volunteers. Volunteers must be knowledgeable about the association, its benefits, and its accomplishments. Some associations use their board members or membership committee members for this reason. Volunteers must be well-trained and supported when making calls to lapsed members.

Finding Good Membership Volunteers

Finding volunteers is increasingly difficult for most organizations today, so association executives have to be more enterprising than ever. The most successful volunteer programs use multiple avenues to promote the opportunities and entice participation.

- *Publicity.* Get the word out to the membership about volunteer opportunities available and how to apply using the association's publications and Web site. Feature active volunteers in the newsletter or on the Web and always include instructions about how to volunteer.

- *Surveys.* Many associations have good success in recruiting new volunteers by surveying their members. There are two approaches. One is to list the committees or volunteer opportunities with a brief description of each. The other is to list topics or issues and/or skills, then use the responses to match the volunteer to the appropriate volunteer opening. In either approach, it is imperative that everyone who returns a survey receive a response and a thank you, even if the assignment they requested is not available.

- *New members.* A welcome telephone call to new members is a terrific time to ask about their interest in becoming active in the association. Usually, the most successful approach with new members is to propose a one-time or limited-time assignment that does not require in-depth knowledge of the association.

- *Talent scouts.* Empower the current volunteers to recruit their colleagues. For instance, it can be part of the job description of every membership committee member to identify at least one potential member for next year's committee.

- *Volunteer job fair.* Take a page from the corporate world and set up a volunteer job fair at an association meeting or conference. Post committee descriptions, preferably augmented by photos of the committees in action (the results they achieved, not multiple shots of people sitting around a conference table!). Committee members should be on hand to answer questions and sign up new volunteers. This can be a fun and creative addition to a standard association reception.

Conclusion

Using volunteers can add a valuable dimension to every membership program. Volunteers help build organizational strength and extend its membership resources. Capitalize on the credibility they can bring to membership programs. In return for their time and energy, volunteers gain recognition, an insider's understanding of the organization, new skills, and a broader professional network.

Keep in mind the special considerations of working with volunteers, and incorporate them appropriately into your planning, recruitment, and retention activities. Investing in a well-planned volunteer program will repay the effort with big dividends in membership loyalty, retention, and growth.

RESOURCES

Books

Connors, Tracy Daniel, ed. *The Volunteer Management Handbook.* New York: John Wiley and Sons, 1999.

Levin, Mark. *The Gift of Leadership: How to Rekindle the Volunteer Spirit in the 21st Century,* 1997. Columbia, MD: BAI.

Schlegel, John F. *Enhancing Committee Effectiveness.* Washington, D.C.: American Society of Association Executives, 1994.

Ellis, Susan J., Jeffrey D. Kahn, and Alan S. Glazer. *From the Top Down: The Executive Role in Volunteer Program Success.* Philadelphia: Energize Books, 1996.

Web sites

American Society of Association Executives
www.asaenet.org

Independent Sector
www.independentsector.org

Ginger Nichols is founder and principal of GinCommGroup, a San Francisco–based consultancy providing consulting and training in strategic planning, membership marketing, and leadership development to associations nationwide. A former chair of the Membership Marketing Section Council, Nichols is an American Society of Association Executives (ASAE) Fellow and serves as dean of the membership program in ASAE's School of Association Management. She can be reached at gnichols@gincomm.com.

CHAPTER SEVEN

Legal Issues

Hugh K. Webster, Esq.

WITH FEW EXCEPTIONS, associations are membership organizations. The relationship of members to their association and the relative rights and responsibilities of each present numerous legal issues in many different areas of the law, including taxation, antitrust, and corporate governance. Many of these issues are important because they strike at the core of what it means to be a voluntary membership association.

Law Governing Associations

A vast majority of associations are nonprofit organizations. *Nonprofit,* of course, does not mean that an association is prevented from making a profit. Rather, it means that the net revenues of an association are not distributed to "stockholders" or members, such as in the form of a dividend. Unlike for-profit companies, associations are not operated to increase the wealth of investors.

Nonprofit status is granted by the state of incorporation of the association. The state nonprofit corporation statute and the court decisions interpreting that statute are primary sources of legal rules regulating associations. State tax laws, including property and sales tax, also are relevant.

From a federal law standpoint, the antitrust law and the tax laws, particularly regarding tax exemption, are of primary importance.

Rights of Members

Basic Rights

Traditionally, two rights are considered basic to the status of a person as a "member" of an organization: the right to vote and the right to hold office. However, the extent and nature of the rights that members may have are defined by the association itself.

The primary sources of rights that belong to a member or category of members within an association are the articles of incorporation and bylaws of the organization. State nonprofit statutes give associations extremely broad, and in many cases completely unfettered, discretion in determining which rights members may have.

If a category of members is designated generally as "voting members," then this typically includes the right to vote for officers and directors; to vote on amendments to the articles of incorporation and bylaws; and to vote in the event of a merger, consolidation, or sale of substantial assets of the association. However, the articles of incorporation or bylaws of the association generally may limit these rights.

Association articles or bylaws are usually explicit with respect to which categories of members are eligible to be elected or appointed to an association office.

It is standard in associations to have different categories of members with different rights attached to each category. Assuming that members within a category are treated equally, there is no legal impediment to such disparate treatment of membership categories.

In sum, the rights of members and the exact definition of those rights are established in the articles of incorporation and/or bylaws of the association.

Governance

As a general rule, members, even voting members, do not have management authority with respect to the association. State nonprofit laws, as well as most association articles of incorporation or bylaws, are clear that management authority rests with the board of directors. Management issues, ranging from establishing the strategic direction of the association to setting dues levels, and everything in between, are solely within the province of the board of directors (unless otherwise explicitly stated in the bylaws or articles of incorporation).

Many state nonprofit laws provide that voting members, generally, may cast a vote "on any matter submitted to the membership at a membership meeting." This is an illusory right, however, because the determination as to whether to submit an issue to a membership vote belongs to the board of directors.

The available methods of recourse for members who are displeased with the actions of their board of directors are to seek to remove board members pursuant to a removal procedure (which will be set forth in the bylaws or in state nonprofit statute), to elect different leaders at the next appropriate time, or to resign their membership. However, members rarely have the ability to dictate management decisions to the board of directors.

Association Records

An association that is tax-exempt is required by law to make available to any member of the public, member or nonmember, copies of its most recent Form 990 information return, as well as the original exemption application of the association. Members have as much right to this data as nonmembers.

However, members also have an additional right under state law to seek certain corporate records. Although state laws differ, the majority allow a member in good standing to demand to review, inspect, and copy corporate records, such as membership lists, board and membership meeting minutes, and financial statements. This generally does not include other corporate records, such as contracts, personnel records, or proprietary information.

In addition, members seeking these documents are required under many state laws to show a *proper purpose*. Courts have defined this term rather broadly, evoking it to block a request for access to records only when it appears that the member wishes to use the information to the detriment of the association (such as to form a competing association);

to gain a commercial advantage (e.g., by using the membership list to market a product or service); or simply to engage in a harassment campaign of the association.

Finally, many state laws require that an annual report of the state of affairs of the association be provided to membership. This may be done at an annual membership business meeting or may be published in the association's magazine or other primary publication annually.

Membership Meetings

Most state nonprofit laws require an organization to hold a membership meeting at least once annually and to provide adequate advance notice thereof. In addition, whether by statute or by association bylaw, elections usually are held during the membership meeting. If an association fails to hold a meeting, then a member may seek to have a court issue an injunction ordering the association to do so.

Membership Criteria

An Antitrust Issue

Antitrust laws are designed to ensure free and unfettered competition in the marketplace. They get their name from their original purpose: to break up the "trusts" or cartels that had been formed in many industries in the late 19th century and that were exercising monopoly power in those markets. Today, antitrust laws are applied more generally to any practice that stifles or harms competition.

Unlike a social club or fraternal organization, membership in an association has economic and financial value to members. Denial of membership, therefore, can have measurable harm to those who are excluded and, thereby, harm competition as well. In this sense, membership restrictions and criteria are an antitrust issue, because the improper exclusion of individuals or companies that are competitors or potential competitors can harm competition. It is also for this reason that associations are not free to adopt whatever membership restrictions they wish or grant or deny membership to whomever they wish.

Certainly, the greater the commercial advantage derived from association membership, the greater the likelihood that the unreasonable exclusion of competitors, either through restrictive membership criteria or discriminatory application of those criteria, may constitute a restraint of trade in violation of antitrust laws. Nevertheless, regardless of the actual extent of competitive advantage that one gains by being a member of a particular association, the best approach for all associations is to adopt only reasonable membership criteria and to apply those criteria in an objective and uniform manner.

An association is not a social club; if a person or company meets the membership criteria, they should be admitted, even if they are not liked by people in the profession or industry.

Permissible Restrictions

Notwithstanding the above, there are certain membership restrictions or criteria that are generally recognized as acceptable. These include:

- function
- geography
- membership in constituent associations
- adherence to association rules

A fundamental membership restriction is one based on function. For example, an association of manufacturers generally can exclude wholesalers and retailers; an association of nurses can exclude doctors. However, the issue can become more complicated if the members of an association do not limit themselves to just one level in the chain of commerce. For example, if members of a manufacturing association also engage in wholesaling or retailing, then it may be difficult to exclude firms that are exclusively wholesalers or retailers, because they compete with the association's general membership.

Geographic restrictions also typically are appropriate as long as they are reasonable, in accordance with the commercial realities in the industry, and do not arbitrarily ignore the realities of the market. Geographic boundaries, for example, that are drawn so narrowly or arbitrarily as to exclude significant competitors may be condemned as unreasonable.

So-called universal membership is another restriction that is generally considered valid. This refers to a requirement that, to join a national association, a member must join regional or local chapters of that association as well.

Finally, a fourth type of generally accepted membership criteria is a requirement that a member adhere to association rules, such as with respect to payment of dues, conformance to bylaws, and compliance with the association's code of conduct or ethics. Violation of such rules by a member is usually adequate grounds for exclusion from membership.

Impermissible Restrictions

There also are types of restrictions that are generally considered to be impermissible. The most basic is any rule designed to exclude competitors. Membership rules that establish exclusive territories and prohibit membership to any firm in an existing member's jurisdiction, for example, will be considered unlawful.

Associations in the past have also attempted to require that members adhere to a particular price schedule or prohibit members from joining competing organizations. These have generally been struck down on antitrust grounds.

What these restrictions have in common is that they suppress competition.

Associations should be careful with respect to membership criteria that involve highly subjective judgments. For example, a membership requirement mandating a "good business reputation" or a "commitment to the profession" certainly could be applied in an arbitrary manner.

Discipline of Members

An association has the inherent authority to discipline a member, including expulsion for cause. Examples of the kind of behavior that might result in discipline include failure to pay dues or abide by other requirements of membership, misuse of the association name or logo, or criminal conduct. Typically, expulsions or other disciplinary actions are provided for in the association bylaws, and courts have long recognized the right of an association to adopt disciplinary rules.

But even when the bylaws or articles of incorporation are silent as to the right to discipline members, courts generally have recognized that the right to do so is inherent in an association. However, it is preferable for an association to explicitly reserve this right to itself, such as in the bylaws or articles of incorporation. This right to discipline extends as well to enforcing codes of ethics.

The primary consideration with respect to discipline is the concept of "due process." At its most basic level, due process means fair proceedings carried on in an atmosphere of good faith and fair play. More specifically, due process involves the following elements:

1. adequate notice of charges and reasonable opportunity to respond to those charges
2. the right to appear before a decision-making tribunal to refute and defend the charges, confront and cross-examine accusers, and make a defense and refute the evidence
3. access to all evidence that may be considered by the decision-making body
4. substantive charges against the member; trivial or trumped-up accusations will not be accepted by a court
5. absence of bad faith
6. adequate evidence of wrongdoing
7. impartiality of decision-makers
8. an appeals process

Self-Regulation

Self-regulation of an industry and profession is a fundamental function of associations, and its benefits and many legitimate purposes are numerous. For example, self-regulation can enhance the reputation of an industry or profession for fair and honest service by establishing standards for doing business and disciplining those who do not abide by those standards.

Nevertheless, self-regulation of a profession or industry through an association is legally sensitive for two reasons. First, self-regulation can be anticompetitive by restricting the ability of members to engage in free and open competition. Second, when rules and regulations under a self-regulatory program are enforced, resulting in either expulsion or other discipline, this can have anticompetitive effects and, therefore, must be carried out in a proper and legal matter.

Any provision of a code of ethics or standards of conduct that affects competitive practices by members is legally suspect and will be carefully scrutinized by a court. Basically, any rule regarding prices or the setting of prices is likely to be struck down as an illegal price-fixing agreement. Similarly, a code provision that restricts the ability of members to engage in competitive bidding will be found to be price fixing. Other code provisions affecting competitive practices that are illegal include rules:

- prohibiting the solicitation of customers that are already using the services or products of another member
- forbidding the submission of price quotations when seeking business
- barring members from offering discounts, premiums, or gifts as a means of attracting customers

Restrictions on how members may advertise their products and services traditionally have been strongly disfavored by federal antitrust regulators. Although price advertising (e.g., how much the products or services are being sold for) is particularly sacrosanct, nonprice advertising generally is also protected as long as it is truthful and nondeceptive. Nonprice advertising restrictions include, for example, requirements that advertisements be "tasteful" or that advertisements not disparage competitors.

With respect to the enforcement of self-regulatory process, the due process rules that apply to discipline of members are equally applicable to enforcement of a code.

Membership Dues

Authority of Associations to Impose Dues
Many state nonprofit corporation statutes specifically provide that an association has the authority to impose dues on its members. This power commonly is set forth in an association's bylaws as well. But even absent

such explicit authority, courts will hold that an association has an inherent right to require the payment of dues, because such income is necessary to the operation of the organization.

However, members have on occasion challenged the authority of an association to impose a special membership assessment, unless such authority is explicitly provided for in the association's bylaws. Although such challenges usually fail, associations should include a provision in their bylaws explicitly authorizing the board of directors to impose an assessment, to remove any doubt in this area.

Different dues levels may be set for different categories of members, and an association has complete authority to determine these levels.

Deductibility as a Business Expense

The IRS and the courts have explicitly ruled that dues payments to an association are deductible by members as a legitimate business expense.

One question that can arise is whether dues paid to an association exempt under section 501(c)(3) of the Internal Revenue Code, as opposed to section 501(c)(6), may be deductible as a charitable contribution. Although a section 501(c)(3) organization may accept contributions that are deductible as charitable contributions by the donor, a member is presumed to be receiving some benefit in return for his or her dues payment and, therefore, cannot take a charitable deduction. But, again, a business deduction is available.

Section 501(c)(6) associations are required by IRS regulations to include a statement on dues invoices that dues are not deductible as charitable contributions. However, a statement may be added that dues are deductible as a business expense. Section 501(c)(3) associations are not required by law to include this disclosure statement.

Effect of Lobbying by the Association

"Lobbying" is generally defined as communications with legislators and their staffs in an attempt to influence legislation or legislative action. The extent that an association engages in lobbying affects the deductibility of dues by members. Specifically, under federal law, no tax deduction is available to members for the portion of membership dues allocated to association lobbying activities. To calculate that "allocable portion," an association is required to determine the percentage of dues income dedicated to lobbying. This same percentage will be the nondeductible amount of the members' dues.

However, associations can adopt an alternative approach, in which the association pays a so-called proxy tax, equal to the highest corporate tax rate, on its legislative expenses for the year. If the association chooses to do this, then the amount of dues paid by members is fully deductible as a business expense.

Unrelated Business Income

Although associations generally are exempt from federal and state income taxation, one significant exception is the so-called unrelated business income tax (UBIT). This tax is imposed on association activities that are considered to be commercial and not substantially related to the tax-exempt purposes of the association.

Two common activities of associations that often result in unrelated taxable income to the association are insurance and advertising. With respect to insurance, both the IRS and the courts have almost uniformly held that providing insurance to members, either directly or through a contractual arrangement between the association and an insurance company, is an unrelated trade or business, and therefore, any net revenue to the association is taxable. Most associations also sell advertising in association publications; this also is almost always classified as an unrelated activity.

Other than the tax liability, in most cases, there are no other adverse consequences to engaging in a commercial venture that is unrelated to the tax-exempt purposes of the association. However, if the unrelated activity or activities become a primary focus of the association, or result in a significant percentage of the association's overall income, this could endanger the tax-exempt status of the association.

One significant exception to the rules on unrelated business income concerns "passive" income. This is income received from an activity that is generally considered to be unrelated, but because the association is not actively involved in that activity, the income is not considered taxable. This is an exception to the UBIT rules. An example would be an insurance arrangement in which the association allows an insurance company to use the association name and logo in connection with promoting its product, but the association plays no other role in the promotion or administration of that insurance program. In this instance, the association's conduct is purely "passive" and, therefore, may escape taxation.

Associate Member Dues

One UBIT issue that affects membership directly is associate member dues.

Many associations have as members firms or individuals, such as suppliers to the industry, who do not qualify as regular members. Associations often establish separate membership categories for such persons, with limited rights. This practice is permissible, but associations should take steps to ensure that associate members bring value to the association and participate in association activities as bona fide members.

Such steps could include, for example, having associate members serve on committees, participate as speakers or moderators at association conferences, and write articles for association publications. Having associate member representation on the association's board of directors and/or giving voting rights to associate members would be the strongest indicators of meaningful involvement of associate members in the association but are not necessary to avoid UBIT.

If the IRS views the associate member category as simply a mechanism whereby the associate members can advertise their products or services to the regular members, then the IRS may treat associate member dues as, in effect, advertising income, which is taxable as unrelated business income.

Liability Issues

Members

Members of associations are analogous to stockholders of for-profit corporations. As such, they are not liable for the debts or other legal obligations of the association. This is true as well with respect to the wrongful acts of the association or of other members, as a general rule. That is, mere membership in an association does not make a member liable or responsible for everything that the association does. However, if a member participates in wrongful conduct or, in some states, is fully aware of wrongful conduct yet does not lodge an objection, then liability may be imposed.

The Association

The question of whether or not an association is liable for the acts of its members is somewhat more complicated. If a member or member representative engages in wrongful conduct and does so ostensibly in the name of the association or while purporting to conduct association business, then the association may be held responsible. This is based on the concept of "implied authority." That is, certain association officials— e.g., directors, officers, committee chairs—may be considered by third parties to be agents or representatives of the association simply by virtue of their positions within the association. Under the law, if it is objectively reasonable to assume such authority or status, then the association may be bound by the acts of these volunteer officials.

For example, if the chair of a standards writing committee were to engage in conduct that violates the antitrust laws in connection with the drafting or interpretation of such standards, then the association could be held legally responsible. Similarly, if an officer or director makes disparaging comments about an association member or industry supplier, the association could be sued for defamation. Finally, if an officer signs a contract for the association, the association likely will be bound by that contract even if the officer had no actual authority to sign.

Subsidiaries

It is not unusual for associations to create wholly-owned subsidiary organizations, either for-profit or nonprofit. This section briefly addresses this issue.

Nonprofit subsidiaries, often referred to as foundations, can be useful to an association for various reasons. For example, if the association is exempt under section 501(c)(6), it may create a section 501(c)(3) foundation to accept charitable contributions for educational or research activity. An association may create a nonprofit subsidiary to operate a particular activity the association wishes to separate out from the parent association, either for political reasons (such as a certification program) or for liability reasons (such as a standards setting function). Typically, the nonprofit subsidiary receives its own tax exemption and is controlled by the parent association through appointment (and removal) of the subsidiary's board members.

For-profit subsidiaries are often formed by associations to conduct a commercial activity that otherwise would be subject to UBIT. An association may also form a for-profit subsidiary if the particular commercial activity has liability issues. Typically, the parent association is the sole or at least the majority stockholder of the for-profit subsidiary and controls the subsidiary through this ownership. An association has to be careful, however, to ensure the separateness of the for-profit subsidiary from the association is maintained. This is done largely through maintaining corporate formalities, such as separate board meetings, minutes, books of account, and so forth.

If revenue from a for-profit subsidiary is paid back to the parent association in the form of a dividend, then it typically will not be taxable to the association. If the money is paid back in some other form, such as rent or royalty, then there may be tax consequences. For a nonprofit subsidiary, there should not be any tax liability for money received by the association parent from the subsidiary. However, if the subsidiary is exempt under section 501(c)(3), and the parent is exempt under section 501(c)(6), then the parent association must be careful when transferring subsidiary funds to the parent. A section 501(c)(3) organization cannot make payments to a section 501(c)(6) entity except in connection with activities that would otherwise qualify as section 501(c)(3)-type activities or for standard items, such as rent.

Federal Election Law

Federal Election Law prohibits corporations, including nonprofit associations, from participating in the election process. For example, associations may not contribute money to candidates for federal office. However, there are certain types of political conduct that associations can engage in vis-a-vis their members.

Specifically, associations may make so-called partisan communications to their members. Such communications might consist of the endorsements of candidates or recommendations that members support certain candidates. If an association has established a political action committee (PAC), it may solicit contributions to that PAC from its membership (and only from its membership). Regarding such solicitations, associations should consult Federal Election Commission regulations on the definition of "member" to make sure that fundraising efforts are directed only to the proper group.

Postal Regulations

Nonprofit organizations are eligible for special reduced postal rates, specifically the nonprofit third class rate. Although Section 501(c)(3) organizations may find it easier to gain approval for such rates, section 501(c)(6) associations likewise can qualify. Although the reduced postal rates can save associations significant sums, there are restrictions on what may be mailed, e.g., materials regarding credit card promotions, insurance products, and travel programs.

Conclusion

Members are the primary constituents of any association. They are also its leaders and its customers. It is not surprising that membership issues are among the most important issues in association law, and they cover the major areas of the law applicable to associations generally, including corporate governance, antitrust, and taxation.

Hugh K. Webster, Esq. is a partner with the law firm of Webster, Chamberlain & Bean in Washington, D.C. He specializes exclusively in the representation of associations and other nonprofit organizations.

About ASAE Publications

The American Society of Association Executives in Washington, DC, is an individual membership organization made up of more than 25,000 association executives and suppliers. Its members manage leading trade associations, individual membership societies, and voluntary organizations across the United States and in 44 countries around the globe. It also represents suppliers of products and services to the association community.

This book is one of the hundreds of titles available through the ASAE Bookstore. ASAE publications keep you a step ahead by providing you and your staff with valuable information resources for executive management, finance, human resources, membership, career management, fundraising, and technology.

A complete catalog of titles is available on the ASAE Web site at **www.asaenet.org** or call the Member Service Center at (202) 371-0940 for the latest printed catalog.

www.asaenet.org

Companion Resource from ASAE

To order ASAE publications, visit the online bookstore at
www.asaenet.org/bookstore or contact the ASAE Member Service
Center by phone (202) 371-0940 or fax (202) 371-8315.

Membership Marketing
Edited by Susan Nicolais, CAE

This companion handbook to *Membership
Operations* provides an in-depth overview of
the issues essential to membership marketing.
It explains the benefits of market research and
discusses the best methods for getting the job
done. Learn to apply marketing to membership
and strategically plan your efforts using the
most current techniques and technology.

This handbook helps take the guesswork out of
determining the best recruitment techniques to
use. In eye-opening sections on retention marketing and renewals, learn how to generate the
best return on investment for your association by:

- tracking your retention rate
- analyzing the results
- adapting your marketing efforts

In the extensive section on developing marketing materials, learn how image,
style, and branding help to ensure the unity of your marketing message. This
book discusses the key factors to consider when producing promotional
material including:

- logos and taglines
- outsourcing
- direct mail
- budget

Authored by seven experts with nearly a century of combined experience in
membership marketing, this book is a must-read for any executive whose job
is to attract and keep members.

2001 • 128 pages • softcover • ISBN 0-88034-176-9
Product #: LST-217404

Other Books from ASAE

To order ASAE publications, visit the online bookstore at **www.asaenet.org/bookstore** or contact the ASAE Member Service Center by phone (202) 371-0940 or fax (202) 371-8315.

Budgeting and Financial Management Handbook for Not-for-Profit Organizations
By Edward J. McMillan, CPA, CAE

Update an obsolete or ineffective budgeting system with a budgeting system that works. McMillan's "Continuous Budgeting" and financial management program is easy to implement and monitor. The book includes sample forms and financial statements, formats for sending budget documents to your approving body, and methods for addressing budget problems.

2000 • 128 pages • softcover • ISBN 0-88034-158-0
Product # LST-216722

The Extraordinary CEO
By Douglas C. Eadie

The "business" of being a CEO is what's left out of most texts on association management. Now in this insightful book, you have a resource that goes beyond mastering the skills required to conduct your association's day-to-day business. *The Extraordinary CEO* lifts you out of the fray to examine how you can diversify and enrich your portfolio of CEO leadership goals, skills, and attributes.

1999 • 96 pages • hardcover • ISBN 0-88034-156-4
Product # LST-216792

Strategic Alliances for Nonprofit Organizations
By Charles E. Bartling, CAE

Bartling uncovers why associations form alliances; what kinds of partnerships associations develop; how to find prospective partners and structure a deal that works; how to avoid the pitfalls of partnerships; how to maintain an effective, ongoing relationship; and how to end the alliance amicably when it no longer serves a worthwhile purpose.

1998 • 93 pages • softcover • ISBN 0-88034-143-2
Product # LST-216760

Other Books from ASAE

Millennium Membership:
How to Attract and Keep Members in the New Marketplace
By Mark Levin, CAE

The needs and expectations of your members are changing
fast. *Millennium Membership* guides you through the steps
you must take to attract and keep members. Topics include
investing in technology, branding, and moving from mass
marketing to mass customization.

2000 • 154 pages • softcover • ISBN 0-88034-163-7
Product # LST-216812

Keeping Members: The Myths and Realities
By Arlene Farber Sirkin and Michael McDermott

Are you recruiting for retention or just one year? *Keeping
Members* redefines membership as the core business for associations and other nonprofit organizations. The authors dispel
12 popular myths about retention and reveal key strategies
for growth, focusing on how CEOs, staff, and volunteers each
have key roles to play in recruiting and keeping members.

1995 • ASAE Foundation • 125 pages • softcover • ISBN 0-88034-099-01
Product #: LST-213551

The National-Chapter Partnership:
A Guide for the Chapter Relations Professional
Edited by James DeLizia

Written for and by chapter relations professionals, this guide
will help you strengthen your national-chapter partnerships.
Each chapter includes a self-assessment for building your
chapter relations program. Ideas are generously illustrated
with samples from other associations. Contents include: The Organization of
Association Chapters. Legal and Tax Considerations. Empowering Chapters
Through Effective Communications. Membership Development. Implementing Government Relations Programs at the Chapter Level. Developing
New Chapters. The Chapter Relations Professional.

1993 • 335 pages • spiralbound • ISBN 0-88034-058-4
Product #: LST-217172